D0981261

GAY HENDRICKS, Ph.D.

The Learning to Love Yourself Workbook

■

A FIRESIDE BOOK
Published by Simon & Schuster
New York London Toronto Sydney Tokyo Singapore

FIRESIDE

Rockefeller Center
1230 Avenue of the Americas
New York, New York 10020

Copyright © 1990 by Gay Hendricks, Ph.D.

FIRESIDE and colophon are registered
trademarks of Simon & Schuster Inc.

Manufactured in the United States of America

10   9

First Fireside Edition 1992

Library of Congress Cataloging
in Publication Data
Hendricks, Gay.
The learning to love yourself workbook /
Gay Hendricks.
p.   cm.
1. Self-acceptance—Problems, exercises, etc.
I. Title.
BF575.S37H45   1990
158'.1—dc20   90-33221
CIP
ISBN: 0-671-76392-X

For Katie, with love and eternal gratitude.

Acknowledgments

I would like to express my deepest appreciation to all the readers of my earlier book, *Learning to Love Yourself*. Thousands have been kind enough to send me letters since the book came out, and many have asked for more activities. Here they are.

I am deeply grateful to four remarkable women who have graced my life, teaching me more than I could ever have dreamed possible about loving myself. These are my wife, Kathlyn; my daughter, Amanda; my mother; Norma Hendricks; and my grandmother, Rebecca Delle Garrett Canaday.

I want to thank John Bradshaw, who uses *Learning to Love Yourself* in his workshops. A deep bow to John for his contribution to our society's healing.

I offer heartfelt thanks and a hug to Sandy Dijkstra, literary agent and miracle worker, and to Kathy and Laurie of her staff.

Finally, I would like to express my gratitude and indebtedness to Thaddeus Golas, whose personal acquaintance has meant a great deal to me over the past few years.

Contents

CHAPTER 1

Making the Commitment to Loving Yourself

INTRODUCTION: WHY YOU SHOULD FOCUS ON LEARNING TO LOVE YOURSELF

Learning to love yourself is a breakthrough that can make every area of life better. In working with more than twenty thousand people during the last two decades, I have come to feel that learning to love yourself is the key movement from which mental, emotional, and even physical health flows. Based on my twenty-some years as a psychologist, and having worked with every mental and emotional difficulty in the book, I can tell you that learning to love yourself is the most powerful therapeutic technique I know of. Even though by now I have written books and given hundreds of talks on the subject, I still feel as passionate and excited about learning to love yourself as I did in that magic moment in 1974 when I first felt love for myself. It is the foundation of everything I do when I work with people, whether I am seeing an individual-therapy client, leading a group, or teaching a workshop. I am continually being moved and reinspired by the power of love to transform. Time and again I have seen this technique cause depressions to lift, relationships to improve, and even longstanding physical illnesses to disappear. If you could only do one thing for your well-being, I would urge you to learn to love yourself.

Many of my clients, however, find it very hard to grant themselves the one or two seconds of unconditional love that makes all these changes begin. In fact, I find that people often wait until the last possible moment before learning to love themselves. They wait until their health has eroded, their relationships are in ruins, and their work is in disarray. I have seen people wait until they are on their deathbeds before opening themselves to love, and I have seen others go to their graves without ever having done so. Does it have to be this way? I don't think so. We would not think of driving a car with the warning lights on for many years until every system was crying out for help or the car became horrendous for us to drive. Likewise, we can learn to spot the early warning signals of a lack of self-love, grant ourselves love, and go on to fulfill our potential. *In the realm of learning to love yourself, a little bit of learning can go a long way.* You might be surprised at how tiny a door you have to open in order to invite in the healing power of love.

This is a time when much healing is required in human relationships. In this area learning to love yourself plays a major role. Human beings tend to demand from others what we are most unwilling to give ourselves. We seek love from others and get mad at them when they do not provide the kind we want. Often we seek love to remedy a lack of love for ourselves. *When we seek love without bathing ourselves in it from within, we will never be satisfied with what we get.* No matter how the love we get is expressed—whether by diamonds or passionate declarations—if it is not matched by our own regard for ourselves it will ultimately make matters worse. I have seen people go to the ends of the earth and to endless specialists seeking a cure for their lack of self-love. They build dream houses, they go on cruises, they consult psychics, and they join crusades—all to get away from the gnawing emptiness inside, the place that can be filled only by learning to love yourself.

WHAT IS LOVE?

Right now, think of someone you love. Think of someone you absolutely know you love, with no conditions or strings attached. Notice the body feeling that goes along with thinking of someone you love. This body feeling of love is exactly the attitude with which we need to embrace ourselves. Perhaps you could not think of someone you love. Then think of something you love. Is it horseback riding? Baseball on a warm summer day? Your pet? Almost all of us have experienced the body sense of love somewhere in our lives. This body feeling of love is the one I want you to cultivate toward yourself.

What do you do if you have never loved or been loved? Some of us do not have any love tracks developed in our minds and bodies. You may try to tune in to the body feeling of love and come up blank. I have noticed that in the workshops I have done on learning to love yourself, about 10 percent of people have this problem. In that case you simply have to invent love. You have to design the feeling of love from scratch, based on the finest type of feeling you can imagine. It can be done. After all, someone originally dreamed up the feeling of love and began calling it by name.

The kind of love that truly enriches people's lives is both tender and tough at the same time. There is a warm, accepting, embracing kind of love that welcomes all, forgives all. This is the type of love you can snuggle up to. We need to embrace ourselves with this kind of love. Then there is the tougher kind of love, the kind that will generate discipline in your life. Imagine that you are in the position of one of my therapy clients. Your husband has asked you to help him stop drinking. After two sober days he wakes you up at midnight. He is sweating and trembling. "Unlock the liquor cabinet," he says. "I've changed my mind. I want a drink." "No," you say. "But I *need* it," he says. "If you really love me you'll open that cabinet."

What do you do? Is it love that makes you give alcohol to an alcoholic? Or is it love that says no and means it, absolutely? In my opinion it is often more loving to be tough, to say no, to set limits. If you do not learn to set limits with yourself and those around you, there will be no room for the more tender, embracing love in your life. In our relationships with our loved ones, and ultimately with ourselves, we must develop this tough, disciplined way of loving ourselves. We must accept ourselves unconditionally, *and* we must demand the very best of ourselves.

So, *learning to love ourselves means developing a warm embrace and a firm hand.* It is learning to treat ourselves with utmost mercy while being merciless in our demand that we be true to our highest ideals. If this sounds like a difficult paradox, so be it. Life is often difficult and maddeningly paradoxical.

HOW IT ACTUALLY FEELS TO LOVE YOURSELF

Perhaps it will help if I share with you some of my own experiences of coming to love myself. The first one that comes to mind as I write is a moment on an airplane a while back. I have been making two and sometimes more airplane trips a month for the past fifteen years, and usually I never even think of being afraid. However, on a trip to Seattle, I felt a wave of fear as we took off and banked steeply. The feeling remained for a few more minutes, while part of my mind wondered, "What's going on here?" I remembered to love myself for feeling afraid. I located the sensations of fear in my body—slight nausea, tight belly muscles, an acrid taste. I relaxed into those sensations and loved them just as I might feel toward my daughter or my wife. I reached out to the fear feelings and surrounded them with the body feeling of love, accepting them. At that moment they ceased. There was no more fear. A split second later I had a realization which explained why I had experienced the wave of fear. I had been feeling so close to my wife lately that I was afraid of dying. I had never experienced so much love and intimacy in my life—I had exceeded my upper limit of how much love I thought I could handle—and so I had imagined the worst that could happen. In my busyness of getting ready for the trip I had failed to acknowledge and process these feelings, so they had to wait until I was comfortably seated on the airplane before knocking on my door. Fortunately, I was able to greet them with love and hear their message. Ten years ago I might have called for a glass of wine to drown them out. Five years ago I might have stuffed myself turgid with a load of airplane food. Now I knew to love my feelings and listen to them.

Another personal example: I have had weight problems since I arrived here on earth. I was an extremely fat baby and the situation didn't improve. I was a fat child, a fat teenager, and a fat young adult—I mean really fat. At my most expanded, I was about a hundred pounds overweight. The story was that I had glandular problems, but that never helped me lose weight, nor did the various pills I was prescribed. Then, in my mid-twenties, I had a series of revelations about myself that resulted in my shedding the weight to my present level, 190 pounds (I am a little over six feet tall). But I still must watch my diet carefully. Too much fat or sugar and I can put on five pounds overnight.

That is exactly what happened to me recently. I was on a speaking tour during which I had no chance to exercise and plenty of opportunities to visit fancy restaurants. But on the next to the last night of the tour I happened to be where there were some scales. I stepped on and was pleasantly surprised to find that I was still the same weight as when I left home. So I used this as an excuse to gorge myself at a wonderful French restaurant. The next day when I got back home I found I had gained five pounds. Either the scales were wrong or I had put on a lot of weight practically overnight. I felt like crying. As those of you over forty may have noticed, it's harder to take it off than when you are twenty or thirty. And it stayed. Two or three days of earnest dieting went by with only a pound or so off. Then I had a realization: I was beating myself up for gaining the weight. What was required was loving discipline, not self-criticism and self-hatred. I stopped in the middle of walking across the room and loved myself for being the weight I was. I located the feelings of self-hate and anger in my body—a squirmy sensation in my chest and stomach—and I loved those feelings just the way they were. I loved myself for hating myself. This brief moment of self-love was the boost I needed. The weight disappeared effortlessly over the next few days.

Learning to love myself has often involved finding something I do not like, something I wish to be rid of, and loving it the way it is. I love myself for wanting to be rid of it, and I love the thing itself. It is really very simple, and it always works. But—and this is a big but—we human beings are so programmed to feel bad about ourselves that we often wait until the last minute before we direct love toward ourselves. Don't wait until a crisis forces you to learn to love yourself. Go ahead. Do it now. You have nothing to lose.

BEFRIENDING AND LOVING YOUR FEELINGS

Human beings are a fountain of feelings. We are always registering fear, anger, sadness, and excitement as the day goes along, whether or not we choose to pay attention to those feelings. There is a delicate balance between how much feeling to let into your consciousness and how much to filter out. Let in too much and you are awash in a sea of emotions, a quivering jellyfish of swirling feelings. Let in too little and you lose touch with your vital energy, becoming a rigid automaton. In learning to handle your feelings effectively, be prepared to spend many years calibrating yourself. You will open up to too much feeling and suffer the consequences; then you may shut too many feelings out of your consciousness and suffer the consequences of that. Think of the automatic pilot on an airplane. The plane drifts; the automatic pilot says, "Going too far to the left—correct by going right." Then the plane drifts too far to the right—"Correct to the left." It does this hundreds of times a minute. The plane is only on exactly the right track a small amount of the time. The rest of the time it is drifting off-center and correcting itself. *The plane gets where it's going by being wrong most of the time.* The same process applies to dealing with our feelings. Few people would be righteous enough to claim that they have a perfect relationship with their feelings. Most of us are in the process of drifting out of touch with our feelings, then correcting by getting back in touch again.

There is no mystery to befriending your feelings. It is simply a learning process. When you first hear a symphony orchestra in a live performance, you may be over-whelmed by the complexity of the sound. Later, as your appreciation of music grows, you may be able to listen selectively—to hear the piccolo or the timpani, for example. Learning to listen to your feelings is a similar process.

Fear is the biggest barrier we need to overcome. We are afraid of the unknown. Unless while growing up we have been encouraged to develop an inner life, we are often in a position of utter ignorance with regard to our feelings. We learned our fear of the unknown through millions of years of evolution. Imagine your small band of cave dwellers huddled around the fire in your cave. You hear an awesome and unfamiliar roar at the mouth of the cave. What is it? Will you eat it, or will it eat you?

Project yourself to one hundred years ago. Your small pioneer family is huddled in your cabin when you hear a strange sound outside. Is it an Indian raid or a grazing buffalo? Project yourself to now. Will the bomb drop? Will the atmosphere turn deathly toxic? Will you get cancer, even if you live a healthy life-style? Human beings have a great deal of practice in fearing the unknown. We carry this fear into our self-inquiry. We become afraid of the contents of our own minds and bodies. In therapy over the years I have heard at least a thousand people say things like:

"If I open up to my feelings it will be like opening Pandora's box."

"If I let myself feel my sadness I'll cry forever."

"If I open up to my anger I'll kill somebody."

"If I let myself feel all my sexual feelings I'll turn into a mad rapist."

We all have to make a leap into the unknown to get to know our feelings. In other cultures where having an inner life is highly valued, children learn early to identify and communicate about their feelings. In these cultures you do not find many headaches, ulcers, or bad dreams. We in Western cultures are only recently catching on to the importance of this skill.

As a therapist, I mainly see people who have capped their feelings up too tightly. A small percentage of my clients are on the other end of the spectrum: they spill their feelings all over themselves and those around them. No matter which end of the spectrum you occupy, take on the project of getting to know yourself and your feelings.

Let me give you a short list of discoveries about feelings I have seen people make in the couple of weeks before I wrote this section:

"I get scared when talking to male authority figures."
"I get angry when I don't get what I want."
"I still feel sad about my husband's death even though it's been twenty years."
"I feel sexual feelings for just about every woman who walks by. But I don't have to act on those feelings or shut them out of my awareness."

Do these sound simple? Of course they are, but so is piloting an airplane or playing the cello. It is simple once you have learned it. Before these people came to learn these simple things, their lives were made unpleasant by being in the dark.

THE UNION OF LOVE AND DISCIPLINE

The most happy and alive people I know are all people who have developed both love and discipline in themselves. They do what they say they are going to do. They keep their commitments, both to themselves and to others. By learning discipline they make more room for love in their lives. If you have not learned discipline, you end up spending much of your time and energy cleaning up messes you have made. This chaos leaves little room for love to grow. Many people have not noticed how much aliveness they cost themselves by not developing discipline, by not keeping their agreements with themselves and others. In chapter 2, you will find several specific activities that are designed to aid you in developing a harmony of love and discipline.

THE MAJOR RESISTANCES TO LEARNING TO LOVE YOURSELF

Most of us have some resistance to loving ourselves; otherwise we would have already learned how. There are some widely shared reasons for not loving yourself. In quire into these with me for a moment.

First, many of us are unwanted from the very moment

of our conception. Some estimate that up to 60 to 65 percent of us are unwanted. For hundreds of years, pregnancy has been greeted with a "let's make the best of a bad situation" attitude. The present generation is the first in history to have a real choice about conception. The fact that almost a million teenagers get pregnant each year in this country means that careful conception is still slow to catch on.

It is possible to be loved but not wanted, wanted but not loved, and neither wanted nor loved. Of course, a fortunate minority of us are both loved and wanted. The circumstances of our conception have a much greater impact on us than we might think. In over twenty years of helping people learn to love themselves in therapy, I have come to have a healthy respect for the impact of our parents' original attitudes toward us. Often in therapy I have asked people to bring in their earliest baby photographs. The looks on parents' faces reveal their attitudes toward the child. I have seen everything from pained stoicism to outright loathing in the photos. People tend to put on a good face for the camera, so one can only speculate at the depth of their negative feelings toward the child.

Later, parental disapproval contributes toward our lack of self-love. Most parents are flawed, some deeply. I have worked with people whose parents put out cigarettes on the soles of the children's feet in a sadistically warped attempt at discipline. For most of us, our parents' disapproval did not run so deep. But learning to disapprove of a child's behavior without disapproving of a child's essential being is a sensitive skill. Many of us, through parental disapproval, came to feel that our very essence was at fault. Our existence here was wrong; our being was a burden on the world around us.

Painful Experiences
Many of us experienced traumas that left us with the conclusion that we were unlovable. We reason, "If this horrible thing is happening to me, there must surely be something wrong with me." One of my psychotherapy clients is a woman who was raped as a teenager by two drunken boys as she walked by a bar after attending a movie by herself. In her misery she replayed the incident dozens of times, berating herself for taking that route toward her car. She consulted her priest, who implied that she was at fault; that if she were not putting out sexual signals it might not have happened. His parting advice was only that if she were pregnant it would be God's will, and it would be a sin to get an abortion. Everywhere she turned, her feelings about herself were made worse. No one simply heard her story and encouraged her to express her feelings. Soon she found that she was losing her hearing, and she went to a physician for help. He failed to ask her what had happened in her life before her hearing started to go. He fitted her with a hearing aid. Finally she found her way to therapy, and was able to work through her complex feelings about the issue. Her hearing came back, but because there had been nothing organically wrong with her ears in the first place, the unnecessary use of the hearing aid had left her with some permanent damage.

The tragedy of this woman, which can still bring tears

to my eyes when I think of her, illustrates a key issue in how we come not to love ourselves. We all experience pain of some degree; this is life. How our pain is received determines whether it will add to our unloving feelings toward ourselves. Suppose the first person she met after her assault simply had taken her in his or her arms and said, "Go ahead. Cry it out. You're angry. You're hurting. I'll help as much as I can." It is rare in life to have our feelings so directly received. And when they are not, we store up the pain inside ourselves. Stored pain distorts our whole experience of life. We see the world differently. Our bodies must adapt to the pain, as do our minds. All this hurt capped up within ourselves makes us less likely to feel good about who we are. *Learning to love yourself, then, is the art of finding a new way to relate to painful experiences.* My client described above, for instance, had to find a new way to relate to this most traumatic experience of her young life. When she came in she said her life was ruined, over. She saw no possibilities for happiness. Her evolution had ceased at eighteen. The first step was welcoming and encouraging her real feelings to come forth. Her religious adviser had not done this, nor had her medical practitioner. So, she had to turn to the relatively new profession of psychotherapy to seek a solution. It often occurs to me in therapy that I am doing a very simple thing for someone that no one else has thought to do. In this woman's case I simply invited her to feel the way she felt about the situation. I did not urge her to accept any beliefs, nor did I fit her with any contraptions to help relieve her symptoms. I said, Tell me how you feel. And she did. The fear, the rage, the hurt came pouring out, and it poured out week after week. When it had ceased to pour, she felt relieved and her hearing returned. No one in the world had heard her, so she had turned off her hearing to blot out the world and its pain. Now someone had listened to her, and in this instance, that was all it took for her body to release its stored pain. It seems so simple, but when I think of how many years it took for me to learn to let myself feel my own feelings. . . .

The Attitudes of Those around Us
Most of us grew up around people who did not feel loving toward themselves. They were burdened, or distracted, or hardened by life's catastrophes; discouragement was a backdrop, fear an undercurrent. They might have been clever at hiding it, but it had its ways of coming forth. When I think of the people I grew up amidst, a certain phrase often comes to mind: They were doing the best they could. They were not malicious, thoughtless, or mean. Life had simply handed them economic depressions, unplanned pregnancies, and the deaths of children by now-eradicated disease. They had done the best they could with it. They had no useful technologies for dealing with pain. Some repressed it, some overate to drown it out, some committed slow suicide with cigarettes and liquor. They had no guardian angels to whisper in their ears, experience your pain and tell the truth about it to someone who can listen nonjudgmentally. All of their life experiences had gradually built up a bank of feeling that could not be penetrated or expressed. Like a permanent cloud of fog, this wall of feeling just sat there, year after

year, finding its way into every nook and corner of their lives. I was aware of this fog bank, but of course could not name it or understand it. Only later did I come to see that it was the sum total of all the unlovable aspects of my family that had been repressed and swallowed.

THE DEVELOPMENT OF OUR TWO PERSONALITIES

Think of yourself as a perfect being with two imperfect personalities wrapped around it. In the middle of yourself is who you truly are. You are essence—pure being—with no conditioning, no programming, no problems. But early in life you had to assemble two different personalities to survive in your environment. These two personalities are by nature imperfect, because they are composed of the best path of action you could think of at a particular time. Within these two major personalities are numerous subpersonalities, which we use to deal with specific situations.

The Birth of Personality One
All of us, in our first year of life, have to figure out what to do for attention. Attention is survival. It brings with it food and the basic caretaking necessary to our lives here on earth during those crucial first days, weeks, and months of life. What most of us have to do for attention is relatively sane and not too difficult. We lie around, goo, cry, crawl a little. For others of us, the task of what to do for attention is more trying. For example, I have seen films of schizophrenic mothers interacting with their

babies. An incredible flaw in their interaction patterns can be observed. When the baby wants to snuggle closely, the mother pushes it away. When it wants to get away, the mother pulls it close. The baby is learning that its basic pulsation of getting close and separating *does not work*. It is learning not to trust its own rhythms. It is learning that to get attention it must sacrifice its own fundamental rhythms to someone else's. Think of how the baby will act in its own close relationships thirty years into the future. It will not know how to get close and how to separate. Sound familiar? This example is dramatic, but we all face similar dilemmas in growing up.

Personality One is built up through learning what it takes to get attention. These lessons continue throughout life, but the crucial ones are determined quite early in life. Think of Personality One as your basic act, the fundamental role you play on the stage of life. Personality One is made up of your relatively benign acts, while Personality Two is more troublesome. Among the popular acts that make up Personality One are: good kid, clown, sports nut, misunderstood genius, and too sensitive. These acts are all relatively benign because they do not cause other people to spend time and money picking up after you. Ultimately, however, these acts are not benign. Later in life you will have to take a close look at how much your act is costing you. We build up an act in order to survive the first twenty years or so of our lives, and then we have to spend the next twenty years dismantling it. Happiness lies beyond our act; so long as we are running our act, we have a screen between us and the world. Acts are about survival, but in adult life you are likely to be interested in more than survival. You likely have the goal of becoming real and feeling complete. It is at this point that you must reassess your act and find out how you are masking your realness with it.

A client of mine came to me at age forty with a classic example of how Personality One can stop working. From earliest childhood he had always been a "nice guy." This act is well received in family and school, and he used it to the maximum. He was mom's helper at home and teacher's favorite at school. Always the class president or treasurer, he was the ever-pleasant kid who could be relied upon. In adult life, however, he came to find that his nice-guy act had a downside. It kept him from knowing his true feelings, some of which were in direct conflict with the nice guy. When he was angry, for example, he buried his feelings because they did not fit his image. Here is a clear example of how our act can interfere with our realness. As he worked through this issue in therapy, he did not become an obnoxious guy (which was one fear that kept him hanging on to his act). He maintained what he liked about being a nice guy, but opened up other parts of him that he was concealing. Then he became a "whole guy," which is really what adulthood is all about.

The Birth of Personality Two
Our second personality, which we wrap around our essence and Personality One, is made up of our strategies for protecting ourselves from pain. For some of us, the pain life hands us is so unendurable and unresolvable that we escape into a more serious act to protect our-

selves from it. Among the acts of Personality Two are: religious zealot, victim, jailbird, gossip, alcoholic. These acts inconvenience other people and society. They also prevent you from ever getting your own real needs met. In Personality Two you are so busy defending yourself that you have no energy for figuring out what you want and how to get it. You end up getting something you don't really want at the expense of other people. Let's look closely at several of the acts of Personality Two, taking the first three I mentioned.

One of my psychotherapy clients had become a religious zealot at the age of twenty-two. By the time he was in his thirties this act had cost him his friendships, a marriage, and his health. The major problem with any act is that *you don't know it's an act while you're doing it.* It simply looks like the way things ought to be. What's more, it looks like the way everyone else ought to be, too. Robert had adopted his religious-zealot act as a response to the unendurable pain of losing someone he loved. His high-school girlfriend dumped him without warning in his early twenties, leaving him for another man. His hopes and dreams had all been pinned on this woman, and when she left he was stunned into a six-month depression. He found his way out of the depression by joining a radically fundamentalist church that preached the sinfulness of just about everything. A particular focus of this church was the extraordinary evil and untrustworthiness of women. This doctrine had great appeal for Robert, and he fell upon it with zeal. Within two years he had risen through the ranks to become a minister of the sect. This religious zealot act dominated Robert's life throughout his twenties. It allowed him to deal with the pain of his loss of love. But the act cost him, because unless pain is dealt with directly it will always take its toll on health, relationships, or on other aspects of life. In Robert's life, it cost him nearly everything. By the time I saw him, Robert was wheezing with asthma and twisted with tension—a walking cauldron of rage and misogyny.

Contrast Robert's act with Suzanne's. She also experienced the pain of a loss, but she adopted a victim act to handle her pain. When Suzanne was five, her parents died in a car crash that she survived with minor scratches. She went to live with an aunt who secretly resented Suzanne's presence and filled her head with much victim programming. To the aunt, Suzanne was always "poor" Suzanne, "poor dear," "you poor thing." Suzanne generalized her victim stance to all of life. By the time I saw her she took no responsibility for anything in her life. She perceived herself as the victim of school, adults, society—you name it.

You may now be thinking: "These acts are themselves painful. How are they protecting the person from pain?" The answer is crucial to understand. Escaping into an act, even one that is lethal, is a way of depersonalizing pain. If I can adopt an act that is *not me*, I can get one step removed from my pain. The act filters the pain through a cloak. For many of us, it is preferable to live once removed from life than to face our pain directly. The act provides a buffer, a short-term solution to the pain that then becomes the long-term problem.

The ultimate extension of the victim act is the jailbird.

One of my acquaintances is a successful professional who was sent to prison early in his career for playing a role in a white-collar crime. As it happened, he was only guilty by association and had not knowingly violated the law, but he was sentenced to a short prison term along with the principal agents of the crime. While in prison, he talked to several hundred prisoners and learned a stunning fact. None of them felt any responsibility for being in prison! Along the same lines, a government agency a while back sent questionnaires to a large number of prisoners in California. The questionnaire simply asked, "What did you do to get in prison, and what could you have done differently to avoid it?" Now, the obvious answers would be something like "I robbed a liquor store to get here, and I could have stayed home that night." But none of the prisoners responded this way. Nobody, in fact, mentioned committing a crime as the reason for being in jail. Most blamed it on their lawyers, some on society, others on their childhood. More prisoners blamed it on their own lawyers than on the prosecutors. Many prisoners blamed it on ungrateful wives and children who let them down by turning them in. The message is clear: Those who take no responsibility end up being locked up in one way or another.

How can prison, undeniably a painful experience, be part of an act that is designed to protect you from pain? If you can set up your life so that you are in a cage, with people telling you when to eat and when to sleep, you can project all your problems onto them. It will look as if the world is really responsible for your pain. And it is, because you won't admit that you are the cause of your problems. You will be able to avoid facing your own pain directly.

LEARNING TO LOVE YOURSELF IN RELATIONSHIPS

The most rigorous proving ground for our self-esteem is the world of close relationships. You can spend years developing a fragile sense of self, only to have it knocked askew by the upraised eyebrow of your lover. If you can learn to love yourself while loving others, you can be proud indeed. It is the Mount Everest of mental health.

Here is the core issue: When you come into closeness with someone else, energy is generated that was not there before. This is, of course, why people get close to each other. Excitement is created; sparks fly. This extra energy brings to the surface Personality One and Personality Two. The act of getting close makes your personality issues come forth. A monk in a cave can meditate for years without being troubled by Personality One or Two, but watch what happens when his former girlfriend drops by the cave for a visit.

At this point a subtle event occurs which has powerful consequences. Since we are in a relationship when Personality One and Two start coming to the surface, it looks like *the other person has caused it*. We think the other person has "made" us feel bad. Instead of thanking them for helping us bring our deeper issues into the light, we blame them for messing up our lives. Instead of saying, "Thank you for putting me in touch with my abandonment issues," we say, "You're gonna leave me, just like all the others." The technical term for this pattern is projection. We become like a movie projector beaming images across the room to the screen; we forget that we are the source of our issues and get caught up in the drama we have projected on the wall. Often we can get through the early stages of a close relationship allowing only Personality One to emerge, but with time Personality Two is sure to come to the fore. At the same time, the other person's Personality Two has arisen, and these two ancient warriors begin to do battle. For example, your victim act may get into a power struggle with the other person's drunk act. Your irresponsible act does battle with your partner's hypercritical role. The cost is enormous. Your creative energy is wasted in power struggles, and you spend so much time defending yourself against pain that you never learn what you really can learn in the relationship. When you are locked in projection you do not remember to focus inwardly to see what you are really feeling and doing. Projection becomes an addiction. Projection, like alcohol, keeps you from focusing on your real inner feelings.

Human beings have twin needs for closeness and for separateness. We have an innate urge to be in union with others and an equally strong urge to develop our own independent selves. Ideally we will develop these two needs to the fullest extent that we are capable. But for many of us, wounds occur either in the getting-close stage or the getting-separate stage. We get close and get left, or we get separate and have an accident. Early in life, many such events occur, leaving tracks in our minds that later influence our behavior in adult relationships. We go into future relationships with a subconscious hope that we can resolve these early issues and really feel close to another human being. At the same time we have developed a set of defenses against the pain that occurred early in life (Personality Two). So, we plunge into a relationship with one foot on the accelerator and the other firmly on the brake.

We have as many defenses against being separate as we do against getting close. For every couple that has arguments when they have opportunities for closeness, there is another couple that has their arguments when they are about to spend some time apart. No matter which direction we are moving in—toward union or autonomy—we are likely to encounter unpleasant aspects of ourselves. And what are we to do when these denizens of our deep past come up to haunt us when we are trying to be close or independent? *Love them!*

Let's look at some of the other alternatives that, while popular, are not very helpful. Many people try to hide Personality Two, sweeping it under the rug and hoping nobody will discover it. It never works. People always notice Personality Two, although they may pretend not to. I have worked with families that pretended for years that Dad wasn't an alcoholic. The act of pretending not to notice cost them as much as the alcoholism. Others run the classic projection pattern, blaming their issues on their partners. A man who fears abandonment may accuse his wife for decades of thinking of leaving him. Projecting it onto her allows him to avoid facing the pain of his own issue. In more than twenty years of practicing psychotherapy, I doubt if a week has gone by when some-one didn't come in with this pattern or one like it.

The only healthy and helpful move we can make when our issues surface is to accept them with love and talk about them lovingly with someone who will listen. If your partner can listen to you with respect, that is wonderful. If not, then you need to find someone, professional or am-ateur, who will listen to you as you describe your personal resistances to getting close and getting separate. Above all, you must cultivate the skill of loving what is within you, rather than hating and hiding it. If you give yourself this task, you will have a rich set of learnings in store for you in the realm of relationships. Hardly a day, or even a minute, will go by without something emerging that needs your love. The payoff is vast. Every time you ex-pand your ability to love yourself, you open yourself to being loved more by others. It could not be otherwise, for love is love, whether you self-administer it or get it from others. Embracing yourself in love allows you to embrace others more lovingly. When you release your foot from the brake and allow yourself to ride free with love, rela-tionships become a joyful dance of loving potential instead of a jerky tug-of-war. We will explore the issues that oc-cur in relationships in more detail in chapter 7.

Now, are you ready to make the commitment to learn-ing to love yourself? Declare it to yourself right now. Say to yourself: *I commit myself totally to learning to love myself.*

Next, find someone to whom you can make a public dec-laration. Call a friend and say: *I've made a commitment to learning to love myself.* If no one is around to call, write a letter to someone you know. Go public. You may inspire others with your commitment to begin his or her own journey to self-love. At the worst he or she may say, "So what?" (And you'll know not to make any more meaningful commitments in that direction.) Going public with your commitment is an important event. It puts you on record as taking a stand for your personal growth. It makes the goal more real to you each time you speak it.

FREQUENTLY ASKED QUESTIONS ABOUT LEARNING TO LOVE YOURSELF

It is normal and natural to have many questions emerge as you work with this material. After all, learning to love yourself is one of the hardest things to master. When I give seminars and lectures on this subject, I always look forward with excitement to the questions from the audience. A really good question can make my day, partly because I enjoy thinking on my feet and partly because a good question is a sign that the participants are being stimulated by the material. In the following section I have compiled a number of the most popular questions that people have asked over the years. I will begin with the all-time greatest-hit question, the one that I have been asked from Austria to Alaska to Asia.

What's the difference between loving myself and being conceited?
Being conceited is an effort to convince others that you are lovable after you have decided you are deeply unlov-

able. When people boast or have a "Look at Me!" sign that they wave, it is invariably because they secretly believe they are not worthwhile. If you really know you are lovable, you give off a natural sense of well-being that needs no advertising. When you feel unlovable, you have to work extra hard to give off the appearance that you are OK. This extra effort is what gives conceit its tackiness.

It seems like an awesome task to learn to love myself, because I've spent so many years hating myself. Is it worth it?
I can hear a lot of despair embedded in this question, and I would urge you to begin simply by loving that despair. When we first begin to wake up in life, whether it's at twenty-five or sixty-five, we sometimes feel like we have a hopeless task in front of us. It's like opening up a closet that hasn't been cleaned in a few decades. At first you may want to shut the door again and run. That's a very hard path, though, because nature does not favor incompletion. If you know there is a task to be done and you ignore it, look out. Your only choice then is to continue to shut out information, which will eventually cause you to shut down. Finally, you begin to see that the only way out is to open the closet wide and turn on the light. Begin at your own pace, one day at a time, to clear up what needs clearing up.

Why is it so much easier to love others than myself?
In the growing-up process we are seldom encouraged to turn love and attention inward. The whole trend of our

early lives is focused toward the outside. Going within is practiced only much later in life, and then only by a small segment of the population. I have worked with people who, though well into adulthood, have never once sat quietly with their eyes closed unless they are sleeping. I find it sad that we give so little encouragement toward developing the skill of inner communion with ourselves. This lack of inner resources sets us up to overvalue the outward direction of our attention. But we all need a balance. Life only works best when our regard for ourselves is absolutely equal to our regard for others. We can only truly love others when we love ourselves.

Aren't there some feelings you don't ever get over? It seems like my grief is bottomless.
There are some feelings that do seem bottomless. The grief over a child's death or the death of any deeply loved one can leave a void that seems immense. It takes time before we can even approach the feeling with our consciousness. It is not wise to think of feelings as things we ever clear out of ourselves. Rather, think of a painful feeling as being like a bonfire in a field. At first it is hot, unapproachable. Later it may still smolder. Even later, you can walk on the ground without pain, but you know there is an essence of the fire that still remains. Take your own time, but be sure to walk over the ground again. You must do so because whatever you run away from runs you. If you find that you resist opening up to any feeling, it's a sure sign that the feeling has an unhealthy grip on you. I remember watching my daughter ride horseback when she was nine or ten years old. The

horse threw her off at one point, and her instructor quickly ran to her side to get her back on the horse as soon as she was able. He knew that if she did not mount again right away, it was likely that she would walk away with an aversion to horses. The same is true with our feelings. As soon as we can, we must approach them again, no matter how painful, and continue our conscious relationship with them.

Is there a danger of getting stuck in my feelings and wallowing in them?
Wallowing in feelings is a sign that you have not opened up to them fully. When feelings are fully felt, they do not last long at all. It is only when we put on the brakes during the process of experiencing a feeling that it feels endless. Go ahead, embrace your feelings fully, and you will find that they pass through like thunderstorms. In sadness, we frequently feel that we will cry forever. In anger, we fear that we will kill someone if we really allow ourselves to feel it. When afraid, we believe that we will be stuck in terminal anxiety if we open the door to it. With sexual feelings, we are afraid that we will become out of control, a danger to polite society, if we fully open to our sexuality. These are all superstitions that our fear sends to us. These superstitions are no more true than any other.

There are some people in my life whom I can't seem to force myself to love. What do I do with them?
First, love yourself for not being able to love them. It may be that the traumas with which they were associated have left feelings in you that you have not dealt

with. There is no need to force yourself to love them; simply love yourself for whatever you feel toward them. Are you angry? Love yourself for feeling angry. Sad? Love that. Whatever you are experiencing is the place to start. The same is true for forgiveness. Never force yourself to forgive. It will come naturally after you have felt the truth of your own feelings. The beautiful feelings like love and forgiveness never come effortfully. They are a gift for us after we have faced the truth.

Is it ever too late? I'm nearly eighty years old and I can't even remember much of my childhood. Do I need to remember it in order to love it?
Just begin by loving yourself for wherever you are. Love yourself for not being able to remember. There is no need to force yourself to think of things from your past. There is always plenty in the present to love. I have worked with people from infants to octogenarians, and I have never found that it was ever too early or too late. Love enriches the present and helps heal the past. It paves the way for a smoother future. I have seen magnificent transformations of people on sickbeds and deathbeds, in very old age. Don't wait, though. Begin now, wherever you are, to love yourself for whatever you feel.

When I try to love myself my attention wanders off to something else. What should I do?
This occurrence is natural. Loving yourself is such a powerful thing that your mind and body can take only a little bit of it at first. It experiences a split second of love, then jumps off to a more trivial subject. It's almost as if our

bodies and minds don't know how to handle this flood of good feeling. This is actually a sign that love is working, though, so keep it up. After a while, you will be able to tolerate more and more, and eventually you may be able to live in a state of continuous positive energy. This state took me many years to attain, but it was worth every moment's time I put into it.

My mask feels like it's been there forever. How do I know there is something real under all my coverups?
Many of us start here. We have worn our masks for so long that they no longer feel like masks: They feel like who we actually are. Begin by loving yourself right where you are, as a mask who doesn't know anything deeper. Appreciate the mask for its role in helping you survive. Then look for a tiny little crack in the mask. Specifically, notice yourself in some situation where you are aware of being your mask instead of your true self. Notice the body feeling that goes along with your mask, and notice what the mask is protecting underneath it. For example, you may be talking to your boss and suddenly you notice that you are caught up in your approval-seeking mask. Notice that underneath this is a deep fear that you are unlovable. Love yourself for your approval seeking and your fear. As soon as you have one tiny experience of loving yourself, the next will come easier.

I say "I love myself" to myself, but I don't really believe it. Do I have to believe it for it to work?
No beliefs required. It is normal to have a doubting reaction when you first introduce the idea of loving your-

self. Remember what happened when the idea that the earth was round was first introduced? The authorities threatened to burn people at the stake for believing such a crazy idea. Our bodies and minds are full of billions of cells that have all survived even though you haven't loved yourself. They don't know yet that you can survive if you love yourself. They're going to resist you. So be patient with this natural process of letting love in. Give yourself plenty of permission to doubt. Let your mind and body have any reaction they want to have, but persevere. Keep working with the idea that you are lovable, and eventually the rest of those billions of cells will catch on that there's a party going on elsewhere in you. They'll want to join the fun.

CHAPTER 2

The Fundamental Learning to Love Yourself Activities

INTRODUCTION: HOW THE ACTIVITIES WORK

All of the following activities have been field-tested in workshops and seminars over the past decade. They have all been found helpful in bringing people into greater love and harmony with themselves. They are to be *done*, not simply read. Reading them probably will be interesting, but I can virtually guarantee that it will not be fully transformative. To experience the remarkable transformative power of these activities, you have to sit down and actually work through them. If you commit yourself to the fifteen minutes or half an hour each activity takes, I guarantee that you will be moved. Thousands of people have made positive alterations in their self-esteem through these simple activities. Join them by giving yourself a half hour a day for the next few weeks to shift the quality of your feelings about yourself.

Some of the activities can be done alone; others require the presence of another person. If you are doing the activities on your own, you will need to tape-record many of them so that you can listen to the instructions. You can recognize the ones you'll need to record because they ask you to close your eyes while you are doing them. In a pinch you can read them to yourself as you do them, but it is much more preferable to listen to them on tape.

One of the most effective ways to do the program is with a buddy system or small group. It is fun to do the activities with others; you will have someone to read the instructions to you and vice versa. Find a friend or two who would like to work through the activities with you. Plot out a schedule of meetings over several weeks. Think of it as a temporary committee formed for the highest of purposes: your well-being now and for the future. Your friends can support you as you dissolve the blocks to loving yourself. Another effective way to do the program is with family members. Many of my therapy clients have worked through the activities with spouses and children. The activities make great family-bonding experiences for those who want to make enhanced self-esteem a family project. I wish I had grown up in a family where these kinds of activities were the norm, and I salute those mothers and fathers whose caring commitment is so large that it can include teaching the whole family how to love themselves more.

I also suggest that you keep a notebook of your reactions to the program. This workbook invites you to write in it from time to time, but some people do not like to mark up their books, and you may wish to use more space than the book allows. A notebook will allow you to keep your workbook clean for future trips through the activities.

You will find some activities easy, others nearly impossible. Everyone's reactions are different. Yours are sacred. If you keep track of your changes, you will have a valuable reference to come back to years from now to see how much progress you have made in your personal evolution. Now, if you are ready to begin this journey, find a quiet place where you can work. My blessings to you as you begin this courageous journey of self-transformation.

ACTIVITY ONE
The First Fundamental
Learning to Love Yourself Activity

This activity will be done in the quiet of your own mind. If you are meeting as a group, do the exercise inside yourself; then discuss your reactions with the others.

Part of the power of this activity is learning what your resistances are to loving yourself. For some people, it is the nagging inner critic who says no to every positive idea they have. For others, their resistance comes at the body level, in the form of tension or pain. Still others experience sleepiness, boredom, or a wandering mind when faced with the possibility of loving themselves. There are no right answers to this activity; just *notice what happens to you*.

If you stick with it long enough to get past your resistance, you may have very positive experiences. At a

Santa Barbara workshop in 1989, some of the participants reported the following reactions to the activity:

> "I felt my chest open and I began to really breathe for the first time."
>
> "I felt a warm light rush up the sides of my face."
>
> ". . . it was like being at the fulcrum of life."
>
> "I had a gentle, peaceful light streaming over my head. I didn't want to come back. I could have stayed there forever."

Instructions
Sit comfortably and close your eyes. Rest inside for about a minute.

Say "I love myself unconditionally" in your mind. Pause for about ten seconds, then repeat this phrase. Continue repeating it, with a ten-second pause between repetitions, until you have repeated it fifteen to twenty times.

During the pause between repetitions, notice what happens in your mind and body. What thoughts spontaneously arise? What body sensations occur? Simply notice your reactions to the phrase "I love myself unconditionally."

After your fifteen to twenty repetitions, rest quietly for a minute, then open your eyes.

Note your reactions in your notebook, and discuss them with anyone present.

Discussion
Your reactions to the phrase "I love myself unconditionally" are always revealing. Did you hear an inner voice

that said "No, you don't!" or a twinge of guilt, or did you have a coughing spell? Did your back start to hurt halfway through or did you get off on a train of thought and forget the whole exercise? No matter what your reaction, it is exactly what needed to happen. It will give you invaluable information about your blocks to loving yourself.

ACTIVITY TWO
The Second Fundamental
Learning to Love Yourself Activity

This activity is an advanced version of the first activity. You will bring the concept of loving yourself outside the confines of your own mind and body to the outside world. Doing so raises the ante, and your reactions will be different, perhaps stronger. Any idea with which you are willing to go public has greater power to transform you than does one you hold privately.

This activity requires a partner. Choose who will go first. After one of you has gone all the way through the activity, switch roles. Save your discussion for after both of you have participated.

Instructions
Stand facing your partner. Choose who will be the talker and who will be the listener first. Stand comfortably, with your arms relaxed at your sides. Place yourselves a comfortable conversational distance apart.

Make eye contact. Notice the quality of your eye contact. Does it feel uncomfortable or comfortable? Continue eye contact throughout the rest of the activity.

If you are the talker, say to your partner the phrase "I love myself unconditionally." Pause as long as it requires you to take three relaxed breaths. Then repeat the phrase "I love myself unconditionally." During the three-breath pause notice your mind and body reactions. Simply breathe and notice, then repeat the phrase. Continue until you have repeated the phrase fifteen to twenty times.

When you have finished, indicate it to your partner and switch roles.

When both of you have finished, enter your reactions in your notebook and discuss them.

Discussion

In more than a decade of watching thousands of people do this activity, I have come to respect its power. I have seen people burst into tears during it, and I have seen them glow with radiant happiness. I have seen several people grow so uncomfortable with it that they wanted to leave the room. I receive letters from people all over the world telling me that this activity alone changed their lives. No matter what your reaction, it will provide valuable information about your process of coming to love yourself. What are the thoughts, feelings, or body sensations that rise up as you say the words of self-love? What do they teach you about what is holding you back from accepting yourself completely?

ACTIVITY THREE
The Third Fundamental
Learning to Love Yourself Activity

This life-changing activity is probably the one that has
yielded the most positive feedback of all the exercises in
the workbook. It seems to touch people universally. You
can do this activity in the quiet of your own mind and
body, although it also can be done in large or small
groups. I have done it with many individual therapy clients in my office and with several hundred people at a
time in hotel ballrooms.

Instructions
Sit comfortably and close your eyes. Take a few deep
breaths and relax your body all over.

Think of someone or some place or thing you absolutely know you love. Picture it in your mind and feel it
in your body. It will likely be a person, but it could also
be a place at the beach or a mountain hideaway or something you love to do. Feel the love in your body. Notice
what this sense of love actually feels like. Where do you
feel it in your body? What are the sensations? Is it warm?
Does it have a shape? a color or a sound? Simply notice
how you experience this love.

When you have a clear feeling of love in your mind
and body, direct the feeling of love toward yourself. Instead of feeling it toward the person, place, or thing,
feel it toward yourself. Shift it over to you. Love yourself just like you love that person, place, or thing you
absolutely know you love. If you lose the sensation, go

back to thinking of the person, place, or thing you love until you can feel it again. Then direct the feeling toward yourself. Feel it all over your body. Relax your mind and let the love into your brain. Feel love for yourself all over.

Continue doing this for several minutes until you feel like resting. Then rest quietly inside for a moment or two before opening your eyes.

Discussion

Reflect on this experience for a few moments. Was it difficult? Did you find it easier to love someone or something outside yourself than to love yourself? Many people do. Whatever your reactions, simply notice them, discuss them with someone, and note them in your notebook.

ACTIVITY FOUR
Transforming Self-Hate to Self-Love

In this activity you have the opportunity to tell the truth about the things you hate about yourself and the world. Be honest. There is nothing to lose. If you have always hated your eyes or your thighs or your size, say so. If you hate the poverty or the violence or the humidity in the world, say so. In order to love yourself and the world around you more clearly, it is helpful first to find out what you do not like about yourself and your surroundings. Many people do not progress to loving themselves because they do not allow themselves to be honest about their dislikes.

Instructions

Get a pen or pencil and two sheets of paper. Label the first sheet "Things I Hate about Myself" and the second sheet "Things I Hate about the World." Working as rapidly as you can, list as many things as you can think of in the next ten minutes. Go back and forth between the two sheets rapidly, brainstorming with no attempt to edit or judge or rationalize. Simply list as many things as you can.

Example:

Things I Hate about Myself

The wrinkles around my eyes
My short legs
The way I'm always getting angry at my kids
My messy desk
The way my hair sticks out in back no matter what I do
    to it

Things I Hate about the World

All the violence
The decline of service in stores
Standing in lines
Air pollution

Continue in this manner for ten minutes. Then put your pen down and read through your list, this time tuning in to the exact feeling each item generates in you. Notice if there are slight variations in feeling or if it's all the same. There are no right answers. Simply notice if there is a difference between how you feel about your eye wrinkles as opposed to the feeling about standing in line. We are interested in finding out if there is a single feeling of hate, or if there are variations and gradations of feeling. When you have discovered to your satisfaction how you experience the feeling of self-hate and hate toward aspects of the world, close your eyes and rest for a moment.

In the quiet of your mind and body, tune in once again to your feelings of self-hate and hate toward aspects of the world. Establish these feelings in your consciousness, then *Love yourself for feeling them. Love yourself for hating yourself and those aspects of the world.*

When you have developed a clear sense of loving yourself for hating yourself and those parts of the world, relax and rest for a few moments before opening your eyes.

Discussion
I was surprised at how much of a difference it made when I learned to love myself for hating myself. Rather than trying to love myself all the time, *I simply loved however I felt, even if it was not positive.* Soon it became more easy to love myself unconditionally. Accepting *what is*, even if it's not pleasant, is an essential first step to changing it. Loving *what is* speeds up the process of change even more. This activity is often difficult for people. I recommend practicing it until you have a fluid ease with loving hate.

ACTIVITY FIVE
From Where You Are to Where You Want to Be

In my therapy work with people over the last two decades, as well as with thousands of people in workshops, I have had the opportunity to assist many people in the process of self-change. I have discovered that there are two crucial moves people must make to initiate change. The first move is to make an unflinchingly honest assessment of the current reality—where they are now—while the second is to develop a clear sense of where they want to go. While this may sound simple, it is not. It is not simple because people frequently have major resistance to looking at exactly where they are and what their goals are. A good bit of my time in therapy with people is spent helping them overcome the barriers to being honest about where they stand and where they want to move.

To look closely at where we are often brings pain that we would rather not scrutinize. To be honest about where we want to go often brings fears of many kinds. What if we are honest about our goals and fall short of reaching them? What if? What if? A dramatic example of this problem is an incident that occurred not long ago in therapy. I worked with an obese woman who said she wanted to lose weight. I simply asked her: How much do you weigh now, and how much do you want to weigh? She did not know the answer to either question. She had not weighed herself in years, and she had consciously avoided looking at herself in a full-body mirror. When she passed a mirror or a shop window she looked the other way to avoid seeing her reflection. When I asked her to step on a scale, she became highly agitated. She made many disparaging remarks about the quality of the scale, saying that it could not possibly give an accurate estimate of her weight. When she finally did weigh herself, she would not look at the numbers. She closed her eyes tightly to shut out the reality.

I encountered more resistance when I attempted to find out where she wanted to be. Among the excuses she gave: that it was metaphysically improper to become attached to goals; that it might be dangerous to her health to set a goal; that God might have a plan for her that involved being fat; that she might become too thin and get sick, etc. What it really boiled down to was that she had associated being fat with her mother's love. Her mother, also obese, had stuffed herself, probably as a substitute for love. She also overfed her daughter and her two sons. All were overweight. To lose weight would be to lose Mom's love. To be slender would be to make Mom's way wrong. So all stayed fat.

This example points out the crucial importance of being bluntly honest with ourselves about where we stand and where we want to go. In this activity, you have the opportunity to generate really meaningful change in your life with a relatively simple process.

Instructions
Get a pen and a sheet of paper. Make two columns. One is titled "Where I Am" and the other is called "Where I Want to Be." Over the next ten minutes, list as many items as you can, from every area of your life. Work

quickly, wasting no time in judgment, criticism, editing, or rationalization. Put every sentence in the present tense.

Example:

Where I Am	*Where I Want to Be*
I weigh 195 pounds.	I weigh 179 pounds.
I have a 1985 Saab.	I have a brand new Saab with automatic transmission.
I have a terrible relationship with my boss and my husband.	My relationships with my boss and husband are satisfying and totally harmonious.
I have a master's degree.	I am enrolled in a Ph.D. program in which I am completely happy.

Continue in this manner for ten minutes. Put the list away for a day or two, then come back to it for another run-through. Do this several times until you have generated a list that is satisfyingly complete.

ACTIVITY SIX
Loving Yourself: A Creative Visualization

Many people are highly visual: They have a strong ability to make pictures in their minds. Others are more auditory, relying on words and sounds for their information processing. Still others are kinesthetic; they feel and sense things in their bodies. In our highly visual culture, where people watch TV two hours a day on the average, the picture is king. If you are one of those people who are good at visualizing, you will appreciate this activity. If you are not skilled at visualization, try it anyway. You may benefit from developing a new area of yourself.

Instructions
Sit quietly and close your eyes. Take a moment or two to relax and get comfortable.

Now picture yourself as if seeing yourself from a distance. Notice the angle from which you are viewing yourself. Are you looking from the front, top, back, side, or some other direction? Are you clothed? If so, what are you wearing? With this image in mind, focus more closely now on parts of yourself that do not feel lovable. These parts may be aspects of your body, mind, feelings, actions, or personality.

Pick one of those unlovable aspects and look at it closely. Zero in on it, observing it as closely as you can. Now bathe it in your love. Think of someone or something that you love, and love yourself with that same love. Surround that part of yourself with love. See your love as a light force that changes that part of yourself. Stay with it until you have a clear picture of your love permeating the formerly unloved aspect of you.

Pick another aspect of yourself that feels unlovable. Look at it closely. Now surround it with love. Bathe it in the light of your love.

Pick another aspect. Again, see it and love it. Watch your love change that part of yourself.

When you feel that you are at a good stopping place, rest for a moment; then slowly open your eyes.

ACTIVITY SEVEN
A Learning to Love Yourself Time Line

In this activity you have the opportunity to make an assessment of your whole life. You will start with your first moment as a conceived being and work forward through time to today. Your object will be to look closely at how you fell out of love with yourself.

Instructions
Take a pen and four sheets of paper. The first sheet will be your time line from conception to birth. The second sheet will cover birth to starting school. The third sheet will be your school years, up through high school. The fourth sheet will be your adult years, from the end of high school to today.

Here is an example of how your first sheet might look:
Conception _____Birth
Mark each point on the time line where any incident occurred that might have had anything at all to do with your ability to love yourself. For example, here is an illustration from my own time line.

Conception___Father dies___+___Mom realizes she's pregnant, goes into depression, stops eating___+ Mom regains ability to eat_____Birth

Continue in this way through each of the four sheets. After you are finished, put your time line away for a week or two. Then get it out again and see if you can add more. Your goal will be to take an unflinching look at the events that may have influenced your self-esteem.

Discuss your time line with someone close. Talking about these events out loud often allows more details to emerge.

ACTIVITY EIGHT
A Letter of Appreciation

In this activity you will step outside yourself to view yourself as an appreciative friend might. Being willing to step free of your usual frame of reference serves an important purpose in life. It allows you to lessen your attachment to how you perceive yourself and the world. Many of the problems we inflict upon ourselves come from getting stuck in our own point of view to the extent that we think that this *is the way it actually is*. It helps to become flexible and fluid, so that you can have a point of view without its having you.

Instructions
Find a quiet place where you can be by yourself for fifteen or twenty minutes. Take a pen and a piece or two of paper.

Write a letter of appreciation to yourself. Begin it with Dear *Your name*, and then write a sincere letter to yourself that details all the things that you can think of that you appreciate. Here are some areas that can be covered: Your body (perhaps for being healthy or skilled at something), your abilities (cooking, writing, gardening), your mind, your actions (volunteer work, kindness to others, getting things done), and your personality.

Here is an example from my files:

> Dear Lou:
> The first thing I want to appreciate about you is your willingness to grow. Many times I've seen you choose learning about yourself and the world over staying entrenched in your opinions. Another thing I want to appreciate is the way you took care of your Aunt Betty during the last year of her life. You called almost every day, and made several visits a week to bring things she liked to the nursing home. You also have a talent for drawing, although you haven't used it in years. Your way of parenting your children is good, too. You are firm without being a dictator. It's not easy raising three kids on your own, but you did a good job of it. Another thing. . . .

Use your own words and creativity to give a detailed portrayal of your positive attributes. When you are finished, put the letter away for a few days, then go over it again to see if you can add anything.

If you have a tape recorder, record your letter when you are finished. Wait a week, then play the letter back to yourself. Doing this will treat your nervous system to an unusual experience: hearing good things about you in your own voice from an outside point of view.

CHAPTER 3

The Self-Discovery Program: A Guided Personal Growth Experience

INTRODUCTION: GETTING STARTED ON THE ROAD TO DISCOVERY

Many of us do not have the luxury of a caring companion or a concerned professional to aid us in our growth. Since *Learning to Love Yourself* came out in the early eighties, I have received many letters from people who were sincerely interested in growth but who did not have the opportunity because of financial, geographical, or other factors. Here is an example from an elderly man, now deceased, who got the book from the county library truck that stopped by his isolated ranch once a month: "I want to learn to love myself before it's too late, but I don't have any family or anybody close to talk to. I live twenty miles from town, which only has a bar and a feed store, anyway. I've spent enough time in the bar to know I'm not going to learn to love myself there. A while back I decided I would spend the last few years of my life trying to figure out who I am. But how do I do it? Where do I start? Do you have any suggestions?"

This chapter is the answer to his letter. It is a guided path to discovering yourself and transforming your self-esteem. It is the guide I wish someone had given me two decades ago when I was starting my own growth path. Many of the awarenesses you can attain through the activities in this chapter are ones that took me literally years to work through on my own. I have tried to compress twenty years of personal growth and therapy experience into this chapter, so take your time in working through it. Many of my clients work with it on and off for a year or so. Others have become so consumed by it that they stayed up late and cranked through it in a week. Whether you do the Self-Discovery Program in small sips or in a big gulp, all I ask is that you do it thoughtfully and with a loving attitude toward yourself.

HOW TO DO THE SELF-DISCOVERY PROGRAM

The program consists of questions and statements that are designed to illuminate key areas of your life. Most people write out their responses to the activities. Space is provided for you to write directly in this book, or you can keep a separate notebook so your book will emerge clean from the process. Two other methods of working through the activities have been used by my clients. The first, for those who do not enjoy writing, is to speak the responses into a tape recorder. The second is to use the activities as a focus of discussion between friends or in a small group. Therapists I have trained run groups based on the activities and have reported that many rich discussions and life changes have resulted.

From time to time as you work through the program you may encounter an activity that does not fit you or for which you can provide no response. For example, an activity may ask you to describe your father's way of dealing with anger and you may never have known your father. You can either skip the activity entirely or do your best to provide a response from things you have heard. Now, if you are ready to begin, get a comfortable, quiet place to work and plunge into the adventure of self-discovery.

Self-Evaluation

What kind of person are you? Describe yourself in less than ten sentences. Be unflinchingly honest in describing your positive and negative qualities. _____

_____

_____

_____

_____

_____

_____

_____

_____

_____

How would the person who knows you *best* and likes you *most* describe you? _____

_____

_____

_____

_____

_____

_____

_____

_____

_____

How would the person who knows you *best* and likes you *least* describe you? _____

_____

_____

_____

_____

_____

_____

_____

_____

_____

_____

What kind of person do you want to be? Describe your ideal self in less than ten sentences, touching on mental, physical, emotional, and spiritual aspects. _____

_____

_____

_____

_____

_____

_____

_____

_____

_____

_____

_____

_____

What do you want? List three things you want in each of the following categories:

Material: _____

_____

_____

_____

_____

_____

_____

Physical: _____

_____

_____

_____

_____

_____

_____

Emotional/Mental: _____

_____

_____

_____

_____

_____

_____

Spiritual: _____

_____

_____

_____

_____

_____

_____

Relationship: _____

_____

_____

_____

_____

_____

In the Very Beginning

Our feelings about ourselves begin very early; some say they begin the day you were conceived. Let's proceed with that working assumption and explore your earliest moments.

When you were conceived, did your mother want to get pregnant? What were her feelings about being pregnant? _____

_____

_____

_____

_____

_____

_____

_____

_____

_____

When you were conceived, did your father want your mother to be pregnant? What were his feelings about becoming a father? _____

_____

_____

_____

_____

_____

_____

During your intrauterine life, did any catastrophic events occur? (Examples: deaths in the family, war, relocation, sickness.) _____

_____

_____

_____

_____

_____

_____

_____

_____

_____

_____

_____

_____

What was your mother's dominant emotional tone during her pregnancy with you? (Examples: happy, sad, excited, angry, resentful, depressed, burdened, scared.)

_____

_____

_____

_____

_____

_____

_____

_____

_____

_____

Describe what you know of your birth. (If you have no knowledge of your birth, see if you can get information from parents or family members. Pay particular attention to complications such as forceps, induced labor, breech birth, cord wrapped around your throat, and extensive use of anesthesia. Recent research on anesthesia, for example, suggests that people who were born to mothers who were heavily anesthetized tend to have a high predisposition toward addictions.) _____

_____

_____

_____

_____

_____

_____

_____

_____

_____

_____

Did you feel bonded to your mother after birth. Did anything occur which interfered with bonding? (Examples: Mother was given heavy anesthesia, incubator was used, complications forced isolation from mother, you were taken away for adoption.) _____

_____

_____

_____

_____

_____

_____

_____

_____

_____

_____

Your Early Life with Your Family

Did anyone in your immediate family resent your being born? (Examples: one or both parents, siblings, grand-parents.) _____

_____

_____

_____

_____

_____

_____

Describe your mother in less than ten sentences. Include positive and negative qualities. _____

_____

_____

_____

_____

_____

_____

_____

_____

Describe your father in less than ten sentences. ____

_____
_____
_____
_____
_____
_____
_____
_____
_____
_____
_____

In what ways are you like your mother and your father? (Cover all aspects: emotional, physical, behavioral, spiritual.) ____

_____
_____
_____
_____
_____
_____
_____
_____
_____
_____
_____
_____

In what ways are you the opposite from your mother and father? _____

_____

_____

_____

_____

_____

_____

_____

_____

_____

Who was the dominant person in the world of your family? Why? (The dominant person might not have lived in your household but may have exerted a powerful influence from a distance or even from the grave.) _____

_____

_____

_____

_____

_____

_____

_____

_____

What was the emotional tone of your family? _____

_____

_____

_____

_____

_____

_____

_____

What did you get from your early family life that
makes you who you are? _____

_____

_____

_____

_____

_____

_____

_____

_____

_____

_____

What did you *not* get from your early family life that
makes you who you are? _____

_____

_____

_____

_____

_____

_____

_____

_____

_____

Looking back on your parents when you were young, what was hidden inside them? (Examples: hurts, fears, discouragement, potentials, grief, the urge to rebel or not conform.) _____

_____

_____

_____

_____

_____

_____

_____

_____

_____

_____

_____

What are your regrets and resentments from your childhood? _____

_____

_____

_____

_____

_____

_____

_____

_____

What or whom from your childhood have you not yet forgiven? _____

_____

_____

_____

_____

_____

_____

_____

_____

_____

_____

_____

What would it take to get you to forgive? _____

_____

_____

_____

_____

_____

_____

_____

_____

_____

_____

Adolescence is usually a time of moving toward independence, often painfully. Describe the first moment you can remember of breaking free from your family. (Example: I remember wanting to sit with my friends at the football games when I got into junior high school, whereas I had always sat with my grandfather before. I remember the hurt in his eyes when I told him, but I did not acknowledge it because I was so uncomfortable with my own feelings.) _____

_____

_____

_____

_____

_____

_____

_____

_____

What were your biggest struggles about as an adolescent? (Example: fighting with your parents about rules, dealing with your emerging sexuality, conflict between pleasing peer group and pleasing parents.) _____

_____

_____

_____

_____

_____

_____

_____

Adolescence is often the time of first love. If you had a big first love as an adolescent, describe what happened to it. Describe any decisions you made as a result of it. (Example: After three years of intense relationship, my big love, Alice, whom I expected to be my life partner, left me and married another man. I was heartbroken, and out of the grief made a resolution never to be in the position of being left again. The effect on my subsequent relationships was that I was always looking for signs of abandonment. At the first sign of betrayal, I bolted.)

What kind of close relationship(s) do you allow now in your life? For example, are your close relationships supportive or critical? Easy or strained? Trustful or suspicious? Helpful or hindering to your overall evolution and success? _____

_____

_____

_____

_____

_____

_____

_____

_____

_____

_____

_____

_____

_____

_____

_____

_____

Are your close relationships absolutely honest? If not, what secrets do you have? _____

_____

_____

_____

_____

_____

_____

_____

_____

_____

_____

How many people around you genuinely care about you? How many people around you do you genuinely care about? Name them. _____

_____

_____

_____

_____

_____

_____

_____

_____

_____

_____

If you could have one person at your deathbed to talk with as you leave this life, who would it be? If you could have three people? _____

_____
_____
_____
_____
_____
_____
_____
_____
_____
_____

Adolescence and early adulthood are the times when you have to learn responsibility. Obviously, many of us put off these lessons until later, and some of us never develop responsibility. Here are some questions to help you see any areas that need work.

In childhood and adolescence, whom or what did you blame for your problems? (Examples: parents, society, genetics.) _____

_____
_____
_____
_____
_____
_____
_____
_____
_____

What responsibilities did you try hardest to avoid? _

_____

_____

_____

_____

_____

_____

_____

_____

Where are you still avoiding responsibility in your life?

_____

_____

_____

_____

_____

_____

_____

_____

What is your attitude toward responsibility? (Example: burden but I have to do it, joy because of freedom it affords, because I haven't lived up to my potential.) _

_____

_____

_____

_____

_____

_____

_____

_____

_____

_____

Feelings

You will have an opportunity to delve deeply into the feeling realm in chapter 4. Use the following questions to give yourself an overview of this crucial area of your life.

Prioritize the following major feelings in terms of how often they occur in your life. Put a *1* beside the most frequently occurring, a *2* by the second most frequently occurring, and so forth.

Anger (irritation, aggravation, annoyance)
Fear (nervousness, anxiety, jitters)
Sadness (grief, hurt, loss)
Guilt (shame)
Happiness (joy, pleasure)

Make a list now of those feelings in the order in which you have prioritized them. Write down several things that trigger each of the feelings. (Example: Fear—being criticized by my boss; driving in fast, heavy traffic; speaking in public.) _____

_____

_____

_____

_____

_____

_____
_____
_____
_____
_____
_____
_____
_____
_____

Make a list of all the people who have hurt you, starting from your very earliest memory. Do not worry about whether these hurts were intentional, whether the person was justified, whether you deserved it, or any other reason. Simply ask yourself: Did I experience hurt? __

_____
_____
_____
_____
_____
_____
_____
_____
_____

How did you deal with your hurt? How do you deal with it now? (Examples: cried, camouflaged it, denied it, turned it into anger.) _____

_____
_____
_____

_____

_____

_____

_____

_____

_____

Hurt is often accompanied by anger. How did you deal with anger in your early life? How do you deal with it now? _____

_____

_____

_____

_____

_____

_____

_____

_____

How did you deal with your fears while growing up? How do you deal with them now? _____

_____

_____

_____

_____

_____

_____

_____

Pleasure and joy are fundamental parts of life. How much do you allow yourself? Are your pleasures healthy, or do they contain a cost? For example, watching a beautiful sunset is pleasurable and has no side effects. Smoking a cigarette may give the smoker pleasure, but it has potentially fatal consequences.

Of the past twenty-four hours, how much of your life has been devoted to healthy pleasures? What were they?

_____
_____
_____
_____
_____
_____
_____
_____
_____

What do you use to block the amount of joy and pleasure you allow yourself in life? (Examples: guilt, worry thoughts, no time for it.) _____

_____
_____
_____
_____
_____
_____
_____
_____

List ten things you can do in the next week that will increase the amount of healthy pleasure in your life. __

_____

_____

_____

_____

_____

_____

_____

_____

_____

Do them!!!

Congratulations. This is the end of the Self-Discovery Program. Your participation is a sign of your commitment to your well-being.

CHAPTER 4

Learning to Love Your Feelings

INTRODUCTION: WHAT WE ALL NEED TO KNOW ABOUT OUR FEELINGS

There is a body of knowledge about our feelings that could literally save lives, and few of us know about it. The breakthroughs over the past two decades in learning to deal with our feelings have been as breathtaking as those in laser technology. These breakthroughs have been made by the community of psychotherapists worldwide, more than a million practitioners working with millions of people. Such advancements have been largely ignored by academic psychology, still hot in the pursuit of rat knowledge and test scores. In my own formal training, I received none—I repeat, *none*—of the most valuable lessons that I use every day to help people relieve their pain. I had to learn everything essential by the seat of my pants, in the process of working with people. These lessons were so fundamental, and in a way so simple, that I could not believe they had been neglected in my formal training.

Intellectual ability is often not helpful in learning about feelings, in fact, it can be a downright barrier. For most of my life I used my intelligence to hide my feelings from myself and those around me. I chose fancy words to obscure my feelings, and clever arguments to keep others away from theirs. The same clever mind that can design computers can also create ulcers through its cunning. An important part of my own evolution has been to create a harmony between my mind and my feelings. It has been a lifelong challenge to allow my feelings, long hidden and very shy, to exist alongside my proud, hungry mind.

Let me give you some examples of the body of knowledge about feelings. In the course of a week I work with numerous people who come into my office in a state of emotional pain and distress. One person may be depressed, speaking slowly and sadly of loss or death. Another person may be jumpy with anxiety or hot with anger. My job is to help them feel better. In addition, I need to help them learn enduring skills that will keep their feelings in a manageable range. So, what I have had to learn are specific techniques that I can use to relieve emotional upset and prevent its recurrence. What can I say or do to help an anxious person relax or a depressed person come up out of torpor? The techniques I am about to share are those which can reliably accomplish these urgent tasks.

The First Principle

Quite possibly the most important thing I do from hour to hour is to encourage people to *be with* their feelings.

In the body of knowledge about feelings, then, the first principle is simply to experience your feelings. By this I mean to tune in to the specific sensations of the feeling. Instead of thinking about the feeling or trying to get rid of it, slow down and let yourself experience it. We ought to learn this simple skill in the first grade. Certainly it should be taught in high school, or at the very least in graduate school. It isn't. You have to learn it the hard way, and many learn it the hardest way imaginable. I have worked with people who have been wrestling with a problem feeling for decades, only to have it go away when I invited them to be with it for a while.

I like to think of feelings as moving through us like rainstorms. Few of us would stand by the window on a rainy day and say things like "It really should not be raining now" and "There's no need for this rain right now." Yet every day many of us carry on a similar monologue inside ourselves with regard to our feelings. We feel fear and quickly squash it with "There's nothing to be afraid of." We get angry and think, "I shouldn't be so upset." We feel sexy and think, "How inappropriate!" What is missing here is the ability to be with our feelings as they pass through, just as we would be with rainstorms.

Feelings are our spontaneous reactions to events like loss, threat, and injustice. They also color your vision, so that if you stay angry long enough, the world will start to look like an angry place. If you dwell in unexplored sadness for a long time, the world will begin to look steadily bleaker. Countless times in therapy people have told me that the world seemed to change before their eyes right after they accessed and released a long-hidden feeling. Feelings, then, are simultaneously a response to the world and a filter through which we see the world.

A human being is a twenty-four-hour-a-day fountain of feelings. Feelings just keep arising, whether or not we are aware of them. If you watch your mind and body closely, you will find yourself concerned with the main fears with which humans have been wrestling for eons: fear of dying, illness, old age, loss of love, criticism, poverty. We try to blot out these fears with liberal doses of food, liquor, and television, but they keep prancing uninvited through our minds and bodies. The same is true of anger and sadness. We may feel angry at injustice, or when our intentions are thwarted. Just as the two-year-old gets angry when a toy is not forthcoming, a fifty-year-old executive may get angry when a promotion isn't given. The fact that we have "civilized" strategies for rationalizing our anger does not make it go away. Sadness follows a similar pattern. It is our response to loss. The loss of love or a loved one through death, divorce, or geographical separation is a theme of life. One of my own life's great sadnesses was the death of my grandmother when I was twenty-one. She was an anchor of love and security, as well as a completely trusted confidante, from my first days on earth throughout my childhood and adolescence. Her death occurred at the height of my ability to repress my feelings, so my grief was incomplete. I felt the enormity of it, but I also had enormous energy invested in hiding all my feelings. Only years later did I come to let myself feel the pain of her loss, and now I still cry about it at least once a month when I find myself thinking about the grandeur of her love and how it shaped my life.

A Second Principle
Every day I help people feel better by teaching them to *breathe with* their feelings. Try it. I predict that you will be amazed by the simple power of a few deep breaths. When in the grip of a feeling, human beings tend to hold their breath. When you *breathe with a feeling, it goes away.* I have seen thousands of people prove this, to their surprise, with a few seconds or minutes of breathing into their feelings rather than holding their breath. Not long ago a woman in her fifties came in with a feeling of depression that had been lingering for months. She could not figure out what it was about, nor could she shake it. She tried exercise and even went back to drinking caffeinated coffee in an attempt to rev herself up. Nothing worked. She tried antidepressants, but they made her drowsy and "not herself." Within the first five minutes of working with her, I made two observations that I quickly pointed out to her. The first was that she looked very angry, although she was concealing it skillfully. When I pointed out what I saw, she immediately burst into tears and told me a number of things she was furious about, none of which she had told anyone. The second observation was that her breathing was upside down. Correct breathing involves allowing the abdomen to relax when you breathe in. The belly relaxes and fills with the in-breath, then flattens with the out-breath. My client had it exactly backward. When she breathed in, she sucked in her abdomen and forced the breath up into

her chest. The problem with this pattern is that it robs your body of oxygen and throws your physiology out of kilter. In fact, if you want to stay in a state of emotional upset all the time, this is the way to breathe. In medical literature this pattern is called chronic hyperventilation, and it is thought to affect a wide variety of illnesses. It took the rest of our first session and half our second session to get her breathing pattern working properly. At first she could not do it. Using all the techniques and tricks I've learned (and which I will show you in the next chapter), we finally got her breathing turned around. Within minutes *her feeling of depression disappeared.* She was astounded, and so was I. While I am accustomed to clients' moods improving with a bit of breath retraining, I had never seen it work so fast. She went out the door like a freshly minted religious convert. She has been using breathing activities you will find in chapter 5 every day for ten minutes, and to date she has not experienced a return of the depressed mood.

A Third Principle

Another important principle about feelings is what I call *telling the microscopic truth.* When you tell the deepest level of truth about a feeling, it often disappears. Here is an example of a dialogue in which I am helping someone learn to tell the microscopic truth.

GAY: How are you feeling right now?
CLIENT: Just upset.
GAY: And where are you feeling the upset in your body?
CLIENT: *(Pause)* I don't know. Sort of everywhere.

GAY: All over your body.

CLIENT: More in my arms and shoulders and neck.

GAY: And in your arms and shoulders and neck, what are the exact sensations you're feeling?

CLIENT: Well, it's kinda tight.

GAY: Tight.

CLIENT: Like part of me wants to punch something and part of me wants to hold back.

GAY: Sounds like part of your tension is anger.

CLIENT: Yeah. I'm angry and I've had to hide it all week.

GAY: And the exact sensations of the anger, what do they feel like?

CLIENT: (*Pause*) Achy, buzzy, a kind of hardness at the back of my neck. My eyes are irritated, too.

(*After this statement, the client takes a deep breath and relaxes. Tears start to form at the corners of his eyes.*)

Telling the microscopic truth has a powerful healing effect. In the example above, very little happened when the client described his feeling as "upset." However, with careful questioning and listening, he was able to get to a very specific description of the sensations as "achy" and "hard." That's when a shift took place. He dropped his tight stance and accessed a deeper level of his being. Telling the microscopic truth *moved* him.

A Key Misconception

One of the most common misconceptions about our feelings is that if we feel something we must act on it. It is essential to our mental health that we build careful separation between our feelings and our actions. It is important to let ourselves feel all our feelings. It is ridiculous to think that we should act on all our feelings. Human beings have been experiencing feelings for thousands of years. We feel fear, anger, and sadness daily, even hourly if we are sensitive enough to notice. If we cut ourselves off from this life stream of feeling we are doomed. Half our existence is gone. If we acted on even a tiny fraction of our feelings, however, we would be doomed, also. Nowhere is this more true than in the realms of anger and sexuality. It is normal to feel anger toward various people and events in life, just as it is normal to feel sexual feelings toward many people and situations in daily life. Yet every week I work with people whose very problem is that they have not allowed themselves to feel anger and sexuality. When I track down the reasons for their repression of these normal emotions, the answer is usually that they stopped feeling because they feared they would have to act on their feelings if they acknowledged them.

So, then, another essential principle of this body of knowledge—the hidden curriculum of life—is that *you can feel all your feelings without having to act on any of them.* Let yourself be with your anger, experiencing it and breathing with it. There is no requirement whatsoever that you do anything with it. The same goes for sexuality. Enjoy all your sexual feelings. After all, human beings wouldn't be here if it weren't for the countless generations of sexy ancestors. If we hang around a tree stump long enough it will start to look sexy! But you must learn to express your sexuality only in ways that bring totally positive consequences to you and others.

In my own life I have had to do major homework on most of the core feelings: anger, sadness, and fear. When I first began to explore myself, I found that I had repressed them all. I was frozen, and my body showed it. I was tense, fat, and dedicated to killing myself with cigarettes. Learning to feel anger, sadness, and fear helped me lose one hundred pounds in a year, quit smoking, and learn how to relax. My blood pressure went from dangerously high to lower than normal in less than a year. As a result of learning to relax my eyes, my vision improved so that I no longer needed glasses. It was an amazing confirmation of the power of held-in feelings to run, and even ruin, my life. While I was trying to restrain all my feelings, *they* controlled *me*. After I learned to feel these emotions, I had them but they no longer had me. It was a crucial shift.

Sadness was the first feeling I accessed. I realized I had not cried in years; in fact, I considered it a sign of weakness. My programming from early on said that feelings were unmanly. Two quotes I remember from childhood: "Big boys don't cry" and "Fear is for pussycats." When I was in my early twenties I lucked upon a fellow teacher at the boarding school where I taught. Neil Marinello was also a graduate student in counseling at a nearby university, and he was in every way the most evolved human being I had ever met. His messages were dramatically different from my programming. He said things like "It's healthy to cry" and "It's all right to be scared" and "Have you ever looked at your anger?" He saved my life. Soon afterward I enrolled in the counseling program (whereas a month before I had not known the field of counseling psychology even existed).

The next year went by in a blur, so fast and furious came the learnings about how hidden feelings had dominated my life. I cried tears about my father's death that I had denied for more than twenty years. I opened up to rage I had hidden under my fat and uncovered fear of practically every aspect of life: fear of death, fear of getting close, fear of my own creativity. In that era I began to write. I needed an outlet for my feelings, and I turned to poetry as a mode of expression. Soon I had published in counseling journals a few poems that caught the eye of a professor at Stanford, where I enrolled the following year for my Ph.D. For me, opening up to my feelings has brought an unbroken chain of positive life experiences, though sometimes the pain of the feeling I am accessing is not fun. I will say, however, that when I open myself fully to experience a feeling, no matter how unpleasant, it never feels bad. Feeling bad is caused by resisting the feeling, not by experiencing it.

The activities in this chapter are designed to help you learn the essentials of how to deal with feelings. You have your own reasons for wanting to do this, but let me suggest a motivation that many people overlook. I think the main purpose of learning the body of knowledge about feelings is *to feel good all the time*. If you learn to notice your feelings, be with them, breathe with them, and tell the microscopic truth about them, it is much more likely that you will feel good all the time. No one knows for sure the purpose of life, but I can guarantee you that it is not to feel bad. Feeling good is your birth-right. Claim your feelings and you will claim your birth-right.

ACTIVITY ONE
Locating Your Feelings in Your Body

A magic healing moment occurs when a person identifies a feeling and locates it in his or her body. I have seen this moment a thousand times and it never fails to move me. Why is this moment so powerful? For the same reason that a sound in the night can be terrifying until you pinpoint its source. You wake up hearing a scraping sound outside. Your heart is pounding. Straining to hear, you suddenly realize that it is the wind causing a tree branch to scrape against the fence. A complete shift oc-curs, and what was terrifying a moment ago now has no effect on your body. Perhaps it's now humorous, or soothing. *When you locate a feeling in time and space, it loses much of its misery-making power.*

This activity will help you relate your feelings to spe-cific sensations. Find a place where you can be quiet and uninterrupted for about fifteen minutes.

Instructions
Sit comfortably and close your eyes. Take a few mo-ments to get used to being inside yourself.

For the next few minutes you will be thinking of cer-tain feelings and noticing how you experience them in your body. The feelings are sadness, anger, and fear.

Each of these feelings has a specific way it affects your body. Certain muscles tense when you are angry, for example, while others tense when you are scared. The more you learn about each of these feelings, the better you will be able to deal with them in real-life situations.

Begin by thinking of sadness. Sadness is about loss and hurt. Right now allow into your mind the memory of a time in your life when you were hurt. When you have it firmly in mind, notice how you feel it in your body. Pay particular attention to the front of your body, down the midline from throat to belly. This is a zone where many people experience their sadness. Notice the sensations in your body that go along with sadness. Think of other times in your life when you have experienced loss, perhaps through death, divorce, or separation. Notice what sensations you feel that accompany those memories. (Continue for two to three minutes.)

Now shift to anger. Anger is often about injustice to yourself and others. It can also be about not getting what you want or need. Think of times in your life when you felt you were treated unfairly. Think of times when you did not get something you wanted or really needed. As these memories come, notice how you experience them in your body. Feel the sensations of anger in your body. Pay attention to the neck and shoulders, as these are areas where many people experience their anger. (Continue for two to three minutes.)

Now shift to fear. Fear is about being threatened. It's not important whether the threat is real or imagined: it feels the same. Think of some of the fears that are common to human beings: death . . . old age . . . being sick

or helpless . . . poverty . . . being criticized . . . losing
the love of someone important to you. As you think of
these fears, notice the sensations in your body. How do
you experience your fear? Many people get jitters in the
stomach, sweaty palms, a nauseous feeling. Just notice
how you experience fear. Notice the specific sensations.
(Continue for two to three minutes.)

When you are going about your daily life, do your best
to tune in to the specific sensations of your feelings. Notice how you experience them in your body. As you become more skilled at locating your feelings in your body,
they will bother you less and less.

Now take a moment or two to rest inside yourself
before opening your eyes again.

Discussion
If you have closed off your feelings for a while, you may
not be able to feel much the first time you do this exercise. If this is the case, come back to the activity every
day or two. With practice you will find that you have an
increased ability to tune in to your feeling sensations.

ACTIVITY TWO
Loving Your Feelings

Now that you have a sense of the body location of your
feelings, let's go to a deeper level: the ability to love
yourself directly for how you feel. As you do this activity, notice which of the feelings gives you the most
trouble. Notice which ones make your mind wander,

which ones you have a hard time thinking of, and so forth.

Instructions

Sit comfortably and close your eyes. Take a moment or two to relax inside yourself.

We will be working with four basic feelings, three of which you explored in the previous activity. The four feelings are sadness, anger, fear, and joy. We will begin with sadness.

Begin by repeating the phrase "I feel sad about _____." Say it a few times, then begin to fill in the blank each time with some event or aspect of your life. For example, you may say, "I feel sad about all the pain in the world" or "I feel sad about my grandfather being in the nursing home" or "I feel sad about the way Bill treats the kids." Do your best to find the real events and issues you feel sad about. Continue with this phrase until you have named at least ten things you feel sad about. When you have reached a good stopping place, tune in to the feeling of sadness in your body. Notice the sensations of sadness and where you feel it. When you have a clear sense of the feeling of sadness, love those sensations. Direct love to the sadness you feel. Love it directly, just as you would love someone in your life you care about deeply. Love this part of yourself as much as you can. (Pause ten to twenty seconds.)

Now shift to anger. Repeat the phrase "I feel angry about _____" in your mind. Each time you say it, fill in the blank with something from your life that you feel angry about. Continue until you have named at least ten things about which you feel angry. When your list is satisfactory, notice how you experience anger in your body. Notice the sensations of anger inside yourself. When you can feel the sensations of anger, love your anger directly. Think of someone or something you love, and love your anger in the same way.

Now shift to fear. Repeat the phrase "I feel scared about _____" Fill in the blank each time with a real fear from your life. Say as many as you can, at least ten. When you reach a good stopping place, tune in to the sensations of fear in your body. Notice where and how you feel fear inside yourself. Now love your fear directly, just as you love a special person or thing in your life. Love your fear completely.

Now shift to joy. Repeat the phrase "I'm happy about _____" Fill in the blank each time with something from your life about which you feel happy. Fill in the blank with at least ten items. When your list feels complete, notice the sensations of happiness in your body. Feel them and bathe them in love. Think of someone or something you love, and give that same love to your happiness.

All parts of you can be loved. As different parts of you emerge during your life, simply love them as you would love someone you care about. Treat yourself as well as you might treat others you love. This goes even for the feeling of hating yourself. Love yourself for hating yourself. That, too, may be a part of you from time to time, and needs to be loved.

Now rest for a moment, then open your eyes.

ACTIVITY THREE
Loving Your Feelings Out Loud

Here is your opportunity to go public with your burgeoning ability to love yourself. It is important to do so. Until you can publicly state your willingness to love yourself, it cannot develop a life of its own. You can begin the process inside, but eventually you have to come out into the outside world and make your commitment live by telling the world.

This activity is best done with a partner. If there is no one around to work with you, stand facing the mirror and say the phrases out loud to your reflection.

Instructions
Pick who is going to be the talker first and who is going to be the listener. The talker sits down; the listener sits facing. When you are ready to begin, the talker simply duplicates the process from the previous activity, but out loud. Begin with sadness, saying out loud "I'm sad about _____," filling in the blank each time with something that you feel sad about. The listener's job is simply to listen. When the talker is finished listing all the things she can think of that she feels sadness about, ask her to pause and love herself.

Move on to anger, fear, and joy. Begin each phrase with the same way: "I'm angry about _____, I'm scared about _____, I'm happy about _____."

When the talker has finished, switch roles.

ACTIVITY FOUR
Getting to Know Your Fears

It is worth investing some extra time in exploring fear. As Bertrand Russell said, "Fear is the main source of superstition, and one of the main sources of cruelty. To conquer fear is the beginning of wisdom." In this activity you will have the opportunity to learn about fear and how it has affected your life. The purpose of the activity is not to make you feel guilty but to help you learn how to *act in spite of your fears*. This message is right at the top of the hit parade of cosmic ideas: Feel your fear and do it anyway. Naturally, there are plenty of things in the world that inspire appropriate fear. A few come quickly to mind: eating unidentified mushrooms in the forest, impugning the masculinity of burly men in a steelworkers' bar, driving while you are drunk, and a thousand others. But most of our daily human fears, the ones that really slow our evolution, are nothing like those very real fears. Most of the things we fear are based on our illusions and distorted perceptions of how the world is. It is as if we construct stacks of thoughts and concepts in our mind, then react to those concepts and thoughts with fear. Under hypnosis, people can be made to salivate to the suggested image of lemon juice. The mere concept of lemon juice is causing real saliva. On the flip side, a concept like the mental picture of someone criticizing you can cause real fear juice (adrenaline) to flow in your body. As the late Alan Watts said, "We're a weird bunch who can't tell the menu from the meal." It is important for us to know that it is our mental concepts that cause our fears, not the intrinsic quality of the feared object. A parish priest from Ireland might be afraid upon meeting the pope. This is because his mental concepts about the pope keep him from seeing the pope as just another person. A New Guinea tribesman who had no mental concepts about the pope would simply see the pontiff as just another guy with a funny hat.

The therapist Fritz Perls said that fear is excitement without the breath. In other words, the very same emotion that we experience as fear could be turned into excitement if we remembered to breathe through it. Before we add the component of breathing, however, let's learn how to take an unflinching look at our fears.

Instructions
Take a sheet of paper and a pencil. Down the left side of your piece of paper, write down the following list of mankind's most primal fears.

I am afraid of dying.
I am afraid of getting old.
I am afraid of illness over which I have no control.
I am afraid of being alone.
I am afraid of being close to people.
I am afraid of losing control.
I am afraid of criticism.
I am afraid of being poor.
I am afraid of losing freedom.
I am afraid of losing love.
I am afraid of _____.
I am afraid of _____.
I am afraid of _____.

Use the last three sentences to write down any personal fears that may be primary for you. For example, if you have a deep fear of snakes or heights or flying or any other aspect of life, write these down. As you write these sentences, check inside yourself to feel how you resonate with each one. Some may be more central to your life than others.

Down the right side of the page, write down the costs to you of each of the fears. Example:

Fear	Cost
I am afraid of being alone.	I overeat when I'm by myself.
I am afraid of losing love.	I am excessively controlling in my marriage.
I am afraid of being poor.	I never spend any money on myself.

Spend fifteen minutes or so compiling as detailed a list as you can of your central fears and their costs. If you can think of absolutely no way that a certain fear applies to you, move on to the next one.

ACTIVITY FIVE
Breathing Through Fears

Fear stops your breathing. This response has been learned through millions of years of evolution. It is an animal's instinct to freeze when scared. This helps it to minimize the chances of being seen, to assess the situation, and to prepare to scram if things look bad. Unlike other animals, human beings have a problem with this behavior. Lower animals will go back to breathing normally after the feared object is gone; humans often keep up their traumatized breathing patterns for years after the feared object is gone from their lives. Let me tell you how I know this.

Frequently in my therapy practice I will see a person whose breathing pattern has been traumatized to the point where the person cannot breathe into a certain part of the body. In healthy breathing, each breathe will make the belly move a lot, and the chest and lower abdomen move a little. If you watch a happy baby breathe, that is what you will see. A traumatized adult may be so frozen that the belly hardly moves, and the chest and lower abdomen not at all. When I help the person learn to breathe normally again, he or she will often have memories and emotional release from the event that traumatized the breathing. I worked with a women in her early twenties who had a severely damaged and restricted breathing rhythm. She had no memories of any events that might have caused that much fear to lodge in her body. After a half hour of helping her establish full, free breathing, she burst into tears spontaneously. Memories of an instance of sexual abuse poured out of her along with the tears. She had completely repressed the incident, which had taken place when she was twelve. Her breathing had been frozen for nearly a decade, and took less than an hour to set right. When I see this sort of thing, and I see it every week, I am always moved by the power of the human organism to change rapidly when the conditions are right.

In the following activity you will learn to breathe while focusing on fear. Learning to do so can have many positive effects on your physical and mental health.

Instructions

(You will need your list of general and personal fears from the last activity.) Sit comfortably and get relaxed. Make sure your clothing or belt is not restricting the movement of your abdomen.

We will begin by learning to relax the muscles of the abdomen as you breathe. This is a very common problem that keeps people from breathing effectively. First, let's explore the difference between what tension feels like and what relaxation feels like. Tense your stomach muscles, focusing on the muscles around your navel. These are the muscles that would tighten if someone were to punch you in the belly. Hold them tightly for a moment. Get a sense of what tension in your belly area feels like. Now relax the muscles completely and take a few deep breaths into your belly. Notice the difference between tension and relaxation.

Now tense your stomach muscles again. Notice the sensations of tension in your stomach. Now relax your stomach muscles again, and notice the difference. Continue tensing and relaxing the stomach muscles every few seconds until you have tightened and relaxed eight to ten times. Then rest.

Do your best to keep your stomach muscles completely relaxed as you work through the rest of the activity.

With a completely relaxed belly, take three deep, slow breaths. Then, pick up your list of fears.

Out loud, say each of the general fears and each personal fear. After you say it, take three deep, slow breaths. For example: Say, "I'm afraid of dying," then take three deep, slow breaths. Then move on to the next fear, until you have stated and breathed with each of the fears on your list. The purpose is to break the old habit of holding your breath when in the presence of fear.

When you are finished: For homework, remind yourself to take three deep, slow breaths several times a day or more often. Particularly, remember to take several deep, slow breaths when you are feeling afraid or upset for any reason. You may be surprised at how much of a difference it makes.

ACTIVITY SIX
Learning to Love Guilt

Most psychological problems are really problems of responsibility. One sizable chunk of the population takes too much responsibility for its actions, while another part takes too little. A few lucky ones have a balance of just enough responsibility. The technical terms for these two approaches are neurosis (taking too much responsibility) and character disorder (taking too little). Most of us tend to one end or the other of this spectrum, though fortunately we do not have the pronounced characteristics that get us into real trouble. The extreme version of the character disorder is found in prison inmates, very few of whom feel responsible for their acts. The extreme version of the neurotic is found eaten up with ulcers or paralyzed by guilt into a dull life without creativity. Those of us in private practice are consulted mainly by people in the normal to neurotic end of the spectrum, while our colleagues in public agencies deal with the character-disorder clients.

I mention all of this because if you are reading this book you are likely to be one of those people who takes too much, rather than too little, responsibility. You may feel responsibility for things that have nothing to do with you, and you may feel guilty about things you never did. I recently ran a stop sign on a lonely country road with the forces of authority nowhere in evidence. Yet another authority was right there with me: I heard my mother's voice chiding me and saw her stern look of disapproval in my mind.

A little bit of guilt is certainly not harmful. It may keep you in line without compromising your health and happiness. But many of us suffer from more than a little bit. No matter where you are on the spectrum, the following activity may help you come to a better understanding of how guilt works in your life. If you experience quite a lot of guilt, this simple exercise may give you genuine relief.

Instructions
Sit comfortably and close your eyes. Take a moment to rest inside yourself.

Begin saying the phrase "I feel guilty" over and over

in your mind. As you do, notice the feelings and sensations that go along with guilt in your mind and body.

Now, each time you say the phrase, fill in the blank with something you feel guilty about: "I feel guilty that _____." For example: "I feel guilty that I don't write to my parents more often" or "I feel guilty that I don't spend more time with my kids." Keep an open mind and let your mind surprise you by filling in the blanks with unexpected guilts. Reach back in time as far as you can go into childhood. (Continue this process for at least five minutes.)

Now notice any sensations and feelings of guilt in your body. Take note of the specific sensations. Where do you feel them? What do they feel like? Establish a clear sense of the feeling of guilt in your body. When it is clear, love that feeling directly. Love it with the same feeling that you would give to someone you really care about. Continue loving the feeling of guilt until you can definitely feel love toward it.

When you get to a good stopping place, rest inside a few moments before opening your eyes.

Discussion and Homework

In the course of working with your guilt, you may find it useful to figure out what you actually owe people. You may have wronged someone, you may have broken agreements that caused hurt, you may have borrowed money that you did not pay back. Or you may have simply been unable or unwilling to tell someone you loved him before he died. All these kinds of events can trigger guilt later. What you can do now is make a list of what you owe and to whom. I did so several years ago, and the results were incredible. I realized there were several people I had not thanked for their influence on me, going back to the time when I was fifteen years old. I wrote notes to them all, even one who took a lot of detective work to find. I found another person to whom I owed a small amount of money. Again, some detective work on my part tracked him down. He was surprised and grateful, because he had hit bottom financially by the time I found him. The personal liberation I felt from this small amount of completing unfinished business has been priceless.

I urge you to take out a piece of paper and make a list of everyone to whom you owe something, whether it is "Thank you" or "I love you" or "Here's the hundred dollars I owe you." Then take action, and watch the magic that happens in your life as a result. If you come up with a debt you cannot repay—a debt to someone who is dead or too ill to recognize your amends, for example—simply acknowledge it and move on.

ACTIVITY SEVEN
Exploring the Feelings of Being Criticized

As children, we often are criticized much more than we are praised. In an ingeniously simple experiment, psychologists attached tape recorders to young children, who then went about their normal day. At the end of the day the researchers took the tapes and analyzed the contents. It turned out that the overwhelming majority of the messages the children received were negative. No wonder we have so much trouble with criticism as adults; one word of reproach and we are replaying the emotions we experienced as children. I once worked with a man who had flown dozens of combat missions in war and had been heavily decorated for his bravery. But when it came to criticism, all it took was one word and he dissolved into a puddle of childhood feeling. He had grown up with a rigid authoritarian father, a general in the military, who was impossible to please. Literally years could go by without a positive word from Dad. Now, in my client's adult life, the old rage and fear about living in constant criticism had finally festered to the point where very little was required to bring it to the surface.

To help you bring out any feelings of criticism that may be influencing your life, work through the following activity. It is best done with a partner, although if you are by yourself you can ask the questions or write them in your notebook.

Instructions
Begin by answering the following questions as honestly as you can. If you are with a partner, designate who will be the questioner and who will be the answerer first. Sit face to face and begin.

Who criticized you most as a child?
Who else criticized you as a child? (Repeat this question until the answerer has exhausted the list of people who criticized him or her.)

What were you criticized most for as a young child before you started school?

What else were you criticized for when you were a young child? (Repeat this question until the answerer has divulged everything he or she can remember being criticized for.)

What were you criticized for most during elementary school?

What else were you criticized for in elementary school? (Repeat as above.)

What were you criticized for most in your teenage years?

What else were you criticized for in your teenage years? (Repeat as above.)

What are you criticized most for now in your life?

What else are you criticized for now in your life? (Repeat as above.)

Now tune in to your sensations of how it feels to be criticized. Notice them, feel them, and give as detailed a description of the sensations as you can.

Now love those sensations and feelings. Love them just as you would love someone you really care about. Love them until you have a clear sense of your love penetrating those feelings.

If you are working with a partner, switch roles now and repeat the activity.

Discussion
When I first began to consider the issue of criticism in my own life I was very surprised to find out how much

energy I had tied up in the subject. When I really began to explore, I saw that my whole existence had been a struggle with criticism, from the moment I was (highly unwantedly) conceived, through the resentment at my birth on the part of my brother and mother, and on through childhood in numerous ways. I reacted to this largely unspoken criticism by tuning people out. In a way this defense was helpful, because I learned to generate my own approval rather than seek it from outside myself. The cost was that I tuned out a lot of potentially useful information as well. Later, as an adult, I compared my perceptions with my brother's, and neither he nor I could remember receiving any praise growing up; criticism was the standard mode of interaction in our family. We had both lived our lives in reaction to criticism. He did so by becoming the ultimate golden boy, while I withdrew inside. Fortunately we both learned from our experience. My brother is one of the best, most positive fathers I've ever seen, and I have done my best to grow in this direction also.

CHAPTER 5

Learning to Love Your Mind

INTRODUCTION: YOUR INTERNAL CRITIC AND THE POWER OF NEGATIVE THINKING

I have heard estimates that we think upward of fifty thousand thoughts a day. This number may go up on a frantic day or down when we are lazing on the beach, but no matter where we are the mind is cranking out spontaneous thoughts day and night. Even as we sleep our minds are churning out thoughts. Researchers distinguish between two types of sleep: REM (for Rapid Eye Movement, during which our eyes are darting back and forth) and non-REM. During REM sleep we are dreaming vivid pictures with plot lines and all the drama one associates with dreams. During non-REM sleep our thought patterns are more basic. If you wake people up during non-REM sleep and ask them what they were dreaming about, they will give you dull answers like "I was thinking of how I need to get my tires checked pretty soon." During REM sleep you will hear a different story:

"I was in my car rolling down a hill toward a big pond, being chased by four men in alligator suits." Day and night, dramatic and factual, thoughts are spewing out of our minds.

Most of us could stand to be on better terms with our fifty thousand thoughts a day. The healthiest attitude to have toward our thoughts is to hold them lovingly but not to get attached to them. If you beat yourself up for the thoughts you have, you will be black and blue by the end of the day. The measure of mental health is how attached you are to your thoughts. Some people are so attached to their thoughts that they do not *have* thoughts, they *are* their thoughts. In other words, we can lose touch with the awareness that our thoughts are just thoughts. We may give them a reality they do not deserve, and act on them as if they were real. In therapy I worked with a couple in which each was absolutely convinced the other was cheating. Their attachment to these thoughts was total. It turned out that these thoughts were completely incorrect, and the true facts of the matter were very revealing. Each had engaged in a secret affair and their thoughts were completely projected.

By contrast, if you hold your thoughts lovingly, just as thoughts, you are much less likely to make yourself miserable. The Buddhists have a wonderful concept that enables them to regard their thoughts in a very healthy way. Their word for the infinite play of the mind is *richness*. Rather than seeing the thought-making activity of the mind as a distraction or a bedevilment, they regard it as evidence of the rich forces of creation. They see their minds as miniature versions of the creative play of the universe. I have traveled in Buddhist countries such as Tibet and Nepal, and I can verify that this attitude works. There is almost none of the anxiety and neurosis you find in other countries. Certainly they have other problems, but neurosis is not one of them.

One fundamental problem of the mind that we will explore together in this section is what I will call your "Internal Critic." Chances are your Internal Critic will be chattering to you as you awaken, and will talk you to sleep at night. In therapy over the years I have worked with thousands of people to identify what makes them unhappy, and most of them have eventually identified an Internal Critic. In most cases, their Critic has been with them since childhood. Your Critic is allergic to self-esteem, self-enjoyment, ease and peace of mind. Your Critic does not want you to feel your feelings, especially the more pleasant ones.

Notice if by now you are starting to dislike your Internal Critic. Yes? *That's exactly what your Critic wants!* Your Critic wants you to criticize yourself for having a Critic. That way it can remain in charge. Your Critic can grab hold of any notion, no matter how enlightening, and turn it into one of its own ploys. Notice now if you are starting to think, "Oh, I guess I should like my Critic." That, too, is a Critic ploy. You see, your Critic loves for you to think in terms of "should" and "ought." By "shoulding" yourself to death you keep yourself from actually focusing on how you feel and what you want. These latter two questions—How do I feel? and What do I want?—are two of the most powerful ways to keep your Internal Critic in its proper place.

The loving attitude toward your Critic is simply to notice it and go on about your business. Your business is figuring out who you are and what you want. Your business is not pleasing the world or controlling others. These are addictions, sometimes more difficult to give up than heroin. Your Critic loves for you to worry about pleasing others and to struggle for control. This keeps your attention focused outward, away from the awarenesses that will bring true growth. If your Critic can keep you focused out there, it can stay in charge. The worst thing you can do with your Critic is to feed it attention, especially negative attention. What puts your Critic in its rightful place is simply to notice dispassionately when it is acting up. You will find a number of very specific ways of accomplishing this in the activities section of the chapter.

After nineteen years of schooling, a few months short of completing my Ph.D., someone finally asked me what I wanted. What did *I* want? The question stunned me into tongue-tied silence. The moment changed my life; in the aftermath of the question I spent days thinking of just what I wanted in my life. Out of that inquiry my whole career developed. In that moment I realized I had done what other people wanted me to do as long as I could remember. When I asked myself, "What do I want?," I got off the trolley tracks of my conditioning and took the risk of determining my life for myself. I have since made it a practice to ask myself the same question every day, and to make sure I ask my clients what they want. When you stop and think about it, considering what you want is a radical move. It overthrows centuries of conditioning. For years we and our ancestors have been told what to want, what to do, and what to think. Perhaps society had to do it this way; after all, human beings are a pretty wild bunch, in need of considerable taming. It was in the fourteenth century, if I remember correctly, that the pope had to issue a bull strictly forbidding sexual intercourse during church services. Some of the parishioners were apparently getting carried away in their religious fervor and allowing it to transport them to new dimensions!

One result of the negative conditioning over the centuries is that many of us find it difficult to know what we want. When I ask people what they want, I get answers like "I don't know" and "Whatever is best" and "It's selfish to think of what I want." Think of the universe as a cosmic waiter. If a waiter came up to take your order in a restaurant you probably would not say, "I don't know what I want" or "I don't want pasta and I don't want chicken and I don't want soup." The waiter could rightfully conclude that maybe you weren't hungry. The universe works the same way. When it comes up to take our order we say, "I don't know what I want" or "I don't want. . . ." Many of us are pretty good at knowing what we don't want, but when it comes to focusing on the positive we get tongue-tied. I frequently get letters from therapy clients who write years later to tell me how things are going. Many of them say that the turning point in their lives—the moment they really began to change—was in the first session when I asked them, "What do you want?"

THE M-A-P (THE MENTAL AWARENESS PROGRAM)

In the next four activities you will develop a skill that could be one of the most important you have ever learned. You will learn to be with the contents of your mind in a whole new way. Rather than criticizing your thoughts or ignoring them or letting them run your life, you will learn to observe them in a relaxed way. Observing your thoughts opens up a new option. With a bit of practice of the following activities you will soon see that your thoughts emerge from a background of space, and they also have space between them. Seeing this space will allow you to become less attached to your thoughts and more identified with the space that is available in your mind. Many people do not know they have any space at all in their minds. It's a jungle up there, or more aptly, it's the Indianapolis 500: speedy, noisy, crowded, fraught with imminent danger. We need to get a friendly relationship going with our thoughts so that we can see the space that will give us more peace of mind. As you practice these activities your mind will get quieter and more spacious.

Among the benefits people have reported from these activities: greater awareness of thoughts and feelings, more peace of mind, relaxation, increased self-esteem, elimination of physical problems such as headaches and insomnia, and heightened ability to concentrate. The more regularly you practice the activities, the more rapidly the results will appear in your life.

The following four activities are done seated comfortably. Most people prefer to practice with their eyes closed, as it brings about a deeper state of relaxation.

Each session, though different, follows a similar theme. The four activities have been carefully sequenced to take you from a fundamental awareness of your mind to a more advanced level of consciousness. Once you learn the activities, you may practice them each day for twenty to thirty minutes.

Ready? Let's begin.

ACTIVITY ONE
The First M-A-P Session

You will first be invited to focus in a specific way on your breathing. You will not be asked to breathe faster or deeper than usual; you will simply follow your breathing as it naturally occurs. Then you will be asked to notice various phenomena as they pass through your mind.

Instructions
Sit comfortably upright. Uncross your arms and legs, and close your eyes if that feels comfortable. Rest for a moment or two. If you wish to practice with your eyes open, keep them softly focused on the ground a few feet in front of you.

Begin by tuning in to your breathing. Do not force it or change it. Simply be lightly aware of your breathing. There are two ways that are especially useful in focusing on your breath. One is to concentrate on the sensations of the breath as it comes in and out of your nostrils. Be aware of those sensations for a moment. (Pause twenty seconds.)

Now place your attention on the rising and falling of your abdomen. Notice the sensations of your breathing as it makes your abdomen rise and fall. (Pause twenty seconds.)

Choose one of those places, nostrils or abdomen, or pick another spot where you can feel the sensations of the breath come and go. Let your awareness rest on this spot, feeling the sensations of the breath as it comes and goes. For the next few minutes, you will simply be noticing the sensations of your breathing. When you find yourself lost in thoughts, simply return your awareness to the sensations of your breathing. The mind will often wander, and there is nothing wrong with that. Whenever you notice it has wandered, simply return to your awareness of your breathing.

(Practice three to five minutes before going on to the next instruction.)

Continue to practice as before, but now make a mental note of "thinking, thinking" when you notice your mind has wandered off into thoughts. When you find yourself thinking instead of being with your breathing, say, "thinking, thinking" to yourself and go back to your breathing. No judgment or censure is implied; simply notice that you are thinking, label it "thinking" and return to the breath. Notice your breathing and your thoughts as you would watch the clouds going across the sky on a summer day, and keep returning your attention to your breathing. Practice now for ten minutes.

(Pause ten minutes.)

Now bring your practice to a close. Simply rest quietly for two minutes before opening your eyes. When your two minutes are up, give yourself a good stretch and go about your normal activities.

ACTIVITY TWO
The Second M-A-P Session

In your first session you learned to use the sensations of breathing as a focal point of awareness. You were asked to be aware of the sensations of the breath, and to return to those sensations when your mind wandered. The wandering of the mind was described as normal and natural; you were invited to note when you were off in thought, then to return to awareness of your breathing.

In this session, you continue to use your breathing as your focus. You will note thinking when it occurs, and you will add a new instruction that will open up the realms of feeling and sensation.

Instructions
Sit comfortably upright. Uncross your arms and legs, and close your eyes if you feel comfortable doing so.

Begin by becoming aware of your breathing. Do not force it or change it. Simply be lightly aware of the sensations of your breath as it comes in and out of your body. Pick a spot where you can feel the sensations—nostrils, abdomen, or elsewhere—and use that as your focal point. When you find yourself thinking, label it "thinking, thinking" and return to the sensations of breathing.

(Practice for five minutes before going on to the next instruction.)

Now we will add a new instruction. Sometimes your mind will wander to a feeling or a sensation. Your mind may focus on tension or pain or simply a pleasant or unpleasant sensation. You might be feeling irritated or angry or scared or sad. When you notice that your awareness has gone to any feeling or sensation, simply note what it is and go back to your breathing. Make a mental note such as "tension, tension" or "pleasant, pleasant" and then return your awareness to the sensations of breathing.

(Practice ten minutes.)

Now bring your practice to a close. Rest for two minutes before opening your eyes. When you are finished, give your body a good stretch and go back to your normal activities.

ACTIVITY THREE
The Third M-A-P Session

In the first two sessions you became aware of the sensations of your breathing as it moved in and out of your body. You used breathing as the focal point of your awareness, and you noted the occurrence of thoughts, feelings, and sensations. When you noticed that your mind had drifted to thoughts or feelings or sensations, you made a note as "thinking" or "pleasant" and returned to the breathing. In this session you will do all of the above as well as add a new dimension of awareness.

Instructions

Sit comfortably upright. Uncross your arms and legs, and close your eyes if you feel comfortable doing so.

Become aware of the sensations of your breathing. Pick a point where you can feel your breathing—nostrils, abdomen, or elsewhere—and use that place as the focal point of your awareness. Don't force or change the breathing. Simply notice it as it occurs. When you find that your mind has wandered to thoughts, make a mental note of "thinking, thinking" and return to your breathing. When you notice that your mind has wandered to sensations or feelings such as tiredness or warmth or anger or happiness, make a mental note of "tired, tired" or "angry, angry" and return to your awareness of breathing.

(Practice for ten minutes before going on.)

Now we will add a new instruction. Notice that your thinking is made up of several different kinds of thoughts. Some thoughts are memories. Others are fantasies, which means thoughts of the future or of things that never happened. Other thoughts are talking, either in your own voice or someone else's. Now, when your mind wanders to a thought, notice what kind it is. Label it "memory, memory" and go back to the breath. Or label it "fantasy, fantasy" or "talk, talk," and return your awareness to your breathing. If you are not sure, use the general label "thinking, thinking" and return to the breath.

(Practice for ten minutes.)

Now bring your practice to a close. Rest for two minutes before opening your eyes. When you are finished, stretch and resume normal activities.

ACTIVITY FOUR
The Final M-A-P Session

In this fourth and final session you will build on all three of the previous sessions by adding the awareness of your Internal Critic.

Instructions
Sit comfortably upright. Uncross your legs and arms, and close your eyes. Rest for a moment inside yourself.

Begin by focusing on your breathing. Simply be aware of your breath as it comes in and out of your body, not changing it or forcing it in any way. Pick a spot where you can feel your breathing sensations, and use that as your place to return your awareness when it wanders off. Whenever you find yourself lost in thought or feeling or sensation, simply make a mental note like "thinking, thinking" or "pleasant, pleasant" or "itching, itching" and return to awareness of breathing. In this session become aware of your Internal Critic. When you notice your Critic activated in any way, label it "critic, critic," then return to your breathing. If you find yourself thinking "You're doing it wrong" or "This is stupid," simply note "critic, critic," and return to the breath. As soon as you notice your Critic is engaged, label it "critic, critic," and go back to the breath.

(Practice for fifteen to twenty minutes.)

When you are finished, rest for two minutes before opening your eyes. Whenever you practice on a daily basis, always give yourself a few minutes after the session to rest before going back into activity. Now, when your rest period is over, give yourself a good stretch and resume your normal activities.

Discussion and Homework
The M-A-P is completely open-ended in the sense that you can add more awareness as your abilities get stronger. With practice, you will see that your mind is often occupied with subtler phenomena, such as intentions and concepts. As your practice gets stronger you will see that your mind has a great deal more space in it than you might have realized. The more closely you can observe the contents of your mind, the more space will open up. A race-car driver can see large gaps between cars even while driving at incredibly high rates of speed, whereas it looks to us in the stands like a noisy blur. As you learn to operate your awareness at higher and higher speeds, you, too, will see that there is a great deal of space between and behind your thoughts. It's not bumper to bumper up there! This awareness can be very liberating. If you can become identified with the space rather than the thoughts, real peace of mind can emerge.

You will notice the most growth if you set aside specific times and practice these activities every day. I have been budgeting forty-five to sixty minutes a day for meditation for over fifteen years now, and I can say without hesitation that it has made everything in my life better. It is the most productive time I spend each day, although from the outside it might look like I am doing nothing. In meditation my mind clears, my thoughts refine and order themselves, and the space is cleared for effective action. Before I began meditating every day I looked busier but did not get as much done. Now I hardly ever look rushed, yet I get infinitely more done than when I was "busy." I urge you to give yourself and those around you the gift of a short period of meditation every day.

ACTIVITY FIVE
Turning Negativity into Positivity

This has been a pivotal activity for many people in helping to turn their lives around. The technique described in the activity represents a brand-new thinking strategy for many people. When you catch on to the power of this technique, I'll bet you will use it every day of your life. Basically, you will be invited to turn your negative mental statements—your complaints—into positive thoughts or requests. You will gradually train your mind to focus on what you want rather than what you don't want or don't have. You will find that turning your mind in a positive direction opens up greater possibilities of getting what you want. This activity has worked magic for many people, and I encourage you to make it part of your life.

Instructions
Take a pencil and a piece of paper. Down the left side of the paper make a list of all the things you can think of that upset you. Include in your list all the personal and universal complaints that you have. Example:

My kids hardly ever call me.
My husband leaves his junk around the house.

There's so much poverty and misery in the world.
I weigh twenty pounds too much.
People are such stupid drivers.

Cover as many as you can in five to ten minutes.

When you are finished with your complaint list, go down the right side of the page, turning each of your complaints into an "I want" statement. Take care to phrase each "I want" statement positively. Instead of saying "I want to lose twenty pounds" or "I want to eliminate all the stupid drivers from the world," say things like "I want to weigh _____ pounds" and "I want everyone I see on the road to drive safely." The above list, for example, could be reworded into the following requests.

I want my kids to call me at least once a week.
I want my husband to keep the house tidy.
I want people in the world to be happy and prosper-
   ous.

Do *not* worry about whether your requests are realistic or possible. This is an exercise in turning your negative thoughts into positive ones. Your requests do not even have to make sense. Just turn each of your negative thoughts into a positive request. Go on to the next instruction when your list has been completely reworded into positive requests.

Sit comfortably, and in the quiet of your mind, say each of your requests to yourself three times. If you are working with a partner, move to the next step, which is to face your partner and to take turns saying each of your requests out loud to each other. If you are working by yourself, face the mirror and deliver each of your requests to your reflection.

Discussion
This activity teaches a skill of enormous importance. Focusing on what you want instead of what you don't want changes everything about the way you think. When you can expand the skill to telling the people around you what you want, you will find that your life moves in vastly more positive directions. I urge you to try this out, even if you think you are basically a positive person. Nearly all of us have dimensions of our lives that could be rendered more positive and effective.

ACTIVITY SIX
Changing Negative Beliefs

Sometimes when I hear my clients tell me about the awful thoughts and negative messages that rattle around in their heads, I say, "What's a nice person like you doing in a mind like that?" None of us begins life with crippling beliefs like "Never show your emotions" or "I must always be in control." But by the time we get to adulthood most of us are saddled with a great deal of excess cognitive baggage. Our belief systems, which we once took on to help us live in the singular world of our families, become the mental barriers we must overcome to live in the real world. I once looked over a list of the major genocidal atrocities that historians had written about over hundreds of years. The list included the ones most of us are familiar with: the Holocaust of European Jewry, the slaughter of millions of women and girls by religious authorities in the witch hunts of the Middle Ages, the Khmer Rouge murder of millions of "Western-tainted" Cambodians. But there were also a dozen or so other major genocides, some involving many millions of people, about which I had never heard. What struck me as I looked at the list was that most of the people had been killed because their beliefs were different from those in power. Beliefs kill. That sentence has an odd ring to it; after all, aren't we supposed to have beliefs? Beliefs are highly regarded as the mental equivalent of motherhood and apple pie. The machinery in our minds seems to thrive on attachment to beliefs; they give us a kind of security that enables the lazy mind to avoid unsettling inquiry. Of course there are plenty of useful, helpful beliefs, and there is no need to throw out the proverbial baby with the bath water. However, the evolving person must examine all of his or her beliefs, to find out which are serving the quest for happiness and which are not. Most of us reading this book are lucky enough to escape being persecuted for our beliefs, but all of us must face the beliefs that are hindering our chances for intimacy with ourselves and others.

This activity will give you the opportunity to explore some of the most common beliefs that create misery in our lives and those around us.

Instructions

Go down this list of common troublesome beliefs, placing a check mark beside each one that you embrace or have embraced at some time in your life.

___ I must not feel angry.

___ I must avoid conflict at all costs.

___ I must not feel afraid.

___ I must not feel sad.

___ I must not feel sexual.

___ I must never express anger.

___ I must never show fear.

___ I must never cry.

___ If things do not go my way, I must be upset about it.

___ I must do everything perfectly, and if I do not I must fret about it.

___ I must grow up quickly, and act like an adult in all situations.

___ There is something wrong with me.

___ I don't deserve love.

___ I must never discuss family problems with outsiders.

___ The world is not a safe place.

___ I must strive for approval in all situations.

___ I must stay in control at all costs.

___ It is unsafe to tell the truth.

Now, list any other negative beliefs that we have not covered that you can see operating in your life.

1. _____
2. _____
3. _____
4. _____
5. _____

Go back through the general list and your specific list, rereading each negative belief. On a separate sheet of paper, turn each of your negative beliefs into a positive statement in your own words. For example, turn "It is unsafe to tell the truth" to something like "I am supported and celebrated for telling the truth in all situations." Always word the statement in an absolutely positive way. If you say "I no longer need to lie," you are still phrasing the belief in a negative way. Word each one so that it is a positive statement of what you can do. This is a good activity on which to get some help from a friend or two. Sometimes it takes a little coaching to reword your negative beliefs in a way that feels motivating to you.

Once your negative beliefs are replaced by positive statements on paper, take them into the real world. Get a friend (or a mirror, if there is no one around) and state each of your new, positive beliefs out loud. Say each one several times until it feels like it's taking hold. If you are working with someone, ask him or her to watch your body language to notice if your body is disagreeing with the new beliefs. Your body probably will fidget and twitch at first (after all, it has survived this long with the old beliefs—why should it give them up?), but stay with each new statement until you have a sense of clarity and agreement with it.

As a homework assignment write each of the new beliefs on a three-by-five card and put the cards around in familiar places: dashboard, mirror, refrigerator. This will help bring your beliefs into action in the world. It will remind you that this wonderful way of thinking and being is available to you.

ACTIVITY SEVEN
Learning to Love Yourself Through Your Dreams

Your mind is a dream factory. Every night you spend an hour or two dreaming, and by age seventy-five you will have spent five years of your life in the dreamworld. No matter how lacking in creative talent we may think we are, each of us is Steven Spielberg in our dreams. I have found a simple technique that can help put your dreams to work in learning to love yourself. It is based on something I learned a long time ago from Gestalt therapy, and I have since modified it to fit some of my own ideas. All you need is a dream in order to participate in this activity. If you have trouble remembering your dreams, put a pad right beside your bed with a pen and light nearby. A dream's richness may fade even minutes after you awaken from it, so there is a value in recording them as soon as you possibly can. When you record your dream for the following activity, do your best to capture as many of the specific images as possible. For example, if you are being chased by a car full of aliens in your dream, notice what color the car is, what model, how many aliens, what they resemble, etc. Instead of writing "I'm being chased by a bunch of aliens in a car," go for a level of specificity like "I'm being chased by four aliens who look like Aunt Frieda in a blue '68 Chevy. I'm racing toward the city dump, which for some reason is full of frogs." Your mind has a reason for each detail of a dream, and trying to see such details clearly can take you further toward a meaningful encounter with this fascinating product of your mind.

Instructions

List each element of your dream on a piece of paper. Be specific, listing each image or element separately. For example, using the above dream:

Blue '68 Chevy
Being chased
Four aliens, all of whom look like Aunt Frieda
Heading toward the city dump
Road is dark, can't see well
City dump is full of frogs

When you have generated your list of images from the dream, complete the following sentence at least *three times* for each image: The _____ represents the part of me that _____. Write the sentence out or say it out loud. I have not found it effective to say it only in your mind. For example, "The *city dump* represents the part of me that's *been dumping all my problems on Aunt Frieda.*" "*Aunt Frieda* is the part of me that's *lonely.*" "The *aliens* are the part of me that's *frightening to myself.*" Analyze each image at least three times, because each time you will come up with a different view of what each image represents. Each dream image has many levels, and it's most useful to brainstorm as many meanings as possible.

Be patient with yourself as you do this part of the activity; sometimes you may get stuck and nothing will come forward. Keep repeating the sentence out loud or on paper until somethings pops out.

When your list of sentences is complete, go through and love yourself for the key part of the second half of each sentence. For example, the key part of the second half of the sentence "Aunt Frieda represents the part of me that's lonely" is the word "lonely." Write on paper or say out loud, "I love myself for being lonely." Do this for each key idea you discovered through completing the sentences.

Discussion

A dream can reveal dozens of hidden meanings that were previously out of reach to the conscious mind. After all, if your conscious mind could have conceived of them, you wouldn't have had to submerge them in the dreamworld. Once, in a therapy session, a woman uncovered thirteen levels of meaning in the dream image of a bridge in a fog. It was the part of her that hated her body, the part of her that was unknown, the part of her that wanted her father's approval, and many others. As she tuned in to these deeper levels of meaning she broke into sobs, accessing a deeper level of emotion than she had previously revealed to herself. This type of deeper learning is the payoff for inquiry into the dreamworld.

CHAPTER 6

Learning to Love Your Body

INTRODUCTION: WHAT WE NEED TO KNOW ABOUT OUR BODIES

There are a host of reasons why we do not love our bodies very much. For one, society holds up ideal bodies for us to compare ourselves to. We look at models on TV and think: I don't look anything like that (but maybe I will if I buy *that* brand of shampoo). The cruel truth is that even the models do not love their bodies very much. I have worked with various show-business personalities in therapy, and I can assure you that their self-regard barely goes skin deep. In fact, some of the most beautiful people with whom I have worked find the greatest flaws in themselves. I was shocked when I first discovered this fact. It made me rethink how I felt about my own body. After all, if these magnificent specimens loathed themselves so much, I thought, is there any hope for the rest of us?

Another reason for our dislike is that many of us have

major flaws in our bodies and in how they function. I found much not to like about my body early in life. For one thing, I was fat. Others ran ahead; I panted behind. In the third grade I was tested and found to have "lazy-eye" syndrome. They wanted me to wear an eye patch and glasses. I pitched a fit about the eye patch, because I didn't want to be the only fat kid in school *and* the only one who looked like a pirate. The net result of all this was that I hated my body, and the feeling did not change until my physical education teacher in tenth grade took an interest in me and helped me get into shape. The real core of the problem did not get touched, however, until much later, in my twenties, when, through therapy and other growth activities, I rediscovered how to love myself.

What are the issues that cause you not to love your body? Is there something wrong with it? Does it look different? Did you hurt it so badly that you never recovered? Even if you do not have any significant body problems like these, there are deep existential issues that show up in the body. The body is where we are most bluntly reminded of our mortality. We labor to get into shape, then find ourselves short of breath after a sedentary week or two. We get sick, we have aches and pains, we have to wash our bodies each day only to have them get dirty again. Yesterday's dark strand of hair is gray today when we look in the mirror. Instead of rejoicing in our increasing wisdom, we panic over our lost youth. In spite of all this, it is possible to learn to love your body. Although we may at times feel like we live in a rusty shack, it is actually the Taj Mahal.

In this chapter I will share with you the most powerful ways I have learned over the years to help people love their bodies. You will learn to see your body as you have never seen it; you will even learn to breathe in a new way. Your body is your home, and if you would like to love where you live, work through these activities with me.

ACTIVITY ONE
The Body Map

Our first task will be to find out how you actually feel about your body. In this activity you will make a map of the trouble spots and the positive spots. It has been helpful to many people to put their bodies on paper; seeing your body as a whole offers you a new perspective. You will need crayons and a body-size piece of paper for this activity. Butcher paper and newsprint are inexpensive and easily obtainable. If you do not have access to a large piece of paper, make a freehand outline of your body on a smaller sheet.

Instructions
Lie down on a body-size piece of paper, and have someone trace around your body.

When your drawing is complete, lightly shade in the parts of you that you don't love in a color that represents negativity to you. For example, if you hate your thighs, color them in with a color you don't like. Around the outside of those areas that you color negatively, spell out what you don't like. You might put "too fat" around your thighs or "too many wrinkles" around your eyes. Spell out all the reasons you don't like particular areas of your body.

When you have colored in all the areas you feel negative about, choose a different color that represents tension. Color in those areas in which you are aware of feeling tension. You will probably put this tension color in at least some of the areas you shaded in before. Around the outside of these areas, write down the situations in which you feel the tension: "when I make a mistake at work," "when my spouse is angry at me."

Choose a different color that represents pain. Lightly shade in the areas in which you feel pain either chronically or now and then. Again, it's all right to have two or more colors in the same area of your body. Around the outside of the painful areas write down the situations in which you experience the pain. It could be "all the time" or "when I'm being criticized" or "when I'm at my desk."

Now choose a color that represents love and positive energy to you. Shade in the parts of your body that you like. Out to the side write a sentence or two about exactly what you like. You might say "My legs are strong" or "I have clear, friendly eyes."

When you are finished, go on to the next part of the exercise.

Put away your drawing materials and sit comfortably with your eyes closed. Pick an area that you colored in as being painful. Be with that place in your body, lightly focusing your attention on it. Feel it, notice it, rest with it. Now go on to another area that is painful. Be with it, focus on it, feel it. Continue until you have focused your attention on all the places you colored as being painful.

Now do the same thing for tension. Go through each spot that you indicated was prone to tension. Pick a place and be with it for a moment. Focus your attention on it, feel it. Then go on to another tense area until you have focused on each one.

Now kindle a positive, loving feeling in yourself. Think of someone or something that you absolutely know you love. Generate this feeling in your body, then direct it toward a part of yourself that you do not love. Love that part, just as you would love a special person or thing. Go through each unloved part of your body, loving it in this manner.

When you are finished, rest comfortably for a little while before opening your eyes again.

ACTIVITY TWO
Body-Trauma Time Line

In this activity you will construct a simple time line of significant events that happened to your body. By doing so, you may gain additional insights about how you came to feel the way you do about your body. I have seen many people react with surprise, even shock, when they see how much they have endured in their bodies. Some of these events are completely the workings of chance. One of my clients was born with a cleft palate, and went through numerous operations to correct it. Other events are more likely self-induced. Another client, one of the most self-hating people I have encountered, had over a dozen major operations over a five-year period before coming to therapy. Regardless of whether our body traumas are self-induced or purely the result of living in a random universe, it is essential that we take responsibility for their effects on our lives. The following activity will allow you to begin the process of finding out how your body consciousness was shaped.

Instructions
Take a piece of paper and draw a line across it. You may need more than one sheet eventually, but begin with one. Beginning with birth, mark each place on the line to indicate significant body events. List illnesses, accidents, scars, and anything else that involved your body. Example:

_____/_____/_____/_____

| 3 months | 2 years | 6 years |
| Got polio | Fell off balcony | Got glasses |

Make your time line as detailed as you possibly can. If you have access to other family members, ask them to remember any events you may have forgotten. Put your time line away for a day or two, then come back to it later. People almost always find that they are able to fill in greater detail if they go through it several times.

When it is complete, go on to the next activity, which uses the time line for further exploration.

ACTIVITY THREE
Learning to Love Your Body Traumas

Now that you have your time line prepared, we will use it to change your attitudes and feelings about those experiences in your life.

Instructions
With your time line close at hand, sit comfortably. Beginning with the most recent entry on your time line, work back through time in the following way: Look at the incident on your time line and then close your eyes and think of all the feelings the incident triggered in you. Take your time to notice all your feelings: fear, anger, sadness, relief, joy, etc. For example, my latest entry was "Hurt my leg playing squash." Some of my feelings about it were: physical pain for several weeks, frustration about not being able to walk or exercise, fears about getting older, and anger that I had pushed myself too hard.

When you are in touch with some of the significant feelings about the event, love yourself for having those feelings. Love yourself for exactly how you felt at that time in your life. Kindle the feeling of love by thinking of someone or something you really love, then direct that feeling toward yourself.

Continue working back through time until you have loved your feelings about the earliest events in your life. For some of these you may have to guess at how you might have felt. For others, you may just have a vague impression of your feelings. Do the best you can to generate an authentic sense of love for your feelings about your body traumas.

ACTIVITY FOUR
The Learning to Love Yourself Breath

I cannot overemphasize the importance of effective breathing. If you learn to breathe effectively, you will feel better physically, emotionally, and mentally. There is a single, central problem that causes many of us to breathe poorly: In brief, we react to stress by tightening our abdominal muscles, forcing our breath up into the chest. Shallow chest breathing is associated with our ancient, primitive mind: the fight-or-flight reflex. I see it in approximately three-fourths of my therapy clients. When they come in their bellies are tight, their breath is labored and shallow, and as a result they are anxious or depressed. I have always, repeat *always*, found the following breathing activities helpful in making the transition to loving yourself. Sometimes they have been life changing. For example, I worked with a woman not long ago who was very depressed. As she told me about her life, I noticed that her chest was barely moving, and her belly not at all. She looked as if she were encased in a tight corset. In addition to helping her work out some of her life issues, I taught her to breathe over the next three sessions. I should say that I helped her rediscover how to breathe, because almost all babies breathe effectively, though by high school most of us have put on our corsets. At the end of the first session, during which she spent twenty minutes breathing effectively, she felt and looked completely different. Color replaced the sallow gray in her cheeks, her eyes had a sparkle instead of a listless dullness, and she even had a hopeful smile on her face. We deepened this new sense of aliveness over the next two sessions, while she practiced the activities (the same ones I will outline for you) at home. At the end of three weeks there was no trace of the depression left. Part of her recovery came from talking about her problems and getting some new solutions, but in my opinion the crucial lesson was in her breathing. Specifically she learned how to breathe diaphragmatically. In healthy breathing, the in-breath should go down into your belly, causing it to expand. The chest moves slightly, but not a lot. Of course, when you are excited or exercising, the chest pumps more actively. In situations in which you are not physically exerting yourself, the breath should be down in your relaxed belly. If your normal state is fear, however, your breathing will be up in your chest even when you are at rest.

A small amount of attention to your breathing will pay off handsomely. You breathe over twenty thousand times a day. If you breathe the way I will show you in the following activities, you can increase the oxygenation of your body by about 5 percent on each breath. Multiply that by twenty thousand, and you have made a world of difference in your mental and physical health. The reason for this difference lies in physiology. You have over 70 percent of your blood circulation in the lower third of your lungs, from the center of your chest down to your navel. Over a quart of blood per minute moves through this area. In your upper chest, you have less than a teacup of blood per minute moving through. In other words, we need to breathe down where the blood is. If we tighten up our bellies, cutting off the flow of breath and circulation, our bodies go into a panic of sorts. This is where the jitters of anxiety and the sluggishness of depression come from. Learning to breathe properly always helps. If you master the diaphragmatic breathing taught in the next two activities, you will make substantial improvements in your well-being.

These activities are very gentle, but before embarking on any exercise program it is wise to check with your physician, particularly if you are being treated for hypertension, stroke, epilepsy, or cardiovascular or respiratory disease. Pay attention to your comfort zone during the activities. They are designed to be done in a relaxed, comfortable way. If you start trying too hard or pushing your breath, you may begin to feel some tension or dizziness. If this happens, simply ease up and rest until the uncomfortable sensations cease. Relax and go back to the activity when the sensations have passed. (In my experience, less than 10 percent of people find that they go beyond their comfort zone during the activities, but if it should happen to you, pause until you are feeling comfortable before resuming.)

For this activity you will need a medium-size book, or something of equal weight and size.

Instructions
Find a quiet place where you can be free of interruptions for the next ten or fifteen minutes. Lie down on your

back and rest for a few moments. Some people find it most comfortable to bring their knees up so that their feet are flat on the ground.

Now place the book on your belly, covering your navel. Close your eyes and tune in to the sensations of the weight of the book. Relax all your muscles as much as you possibly can.

Now, begin to breathe so that you make the book rise on your in breath. Keep your abdominal muscles very relaxed. Feel the book rise on your in breath and come back down on your out breath. Make it very gentle and easy. Don't force or push. Breathe like the ocean waves coming in and going out at the beach. Deep, slow, full breaths, making the book rise and fall. Continue with this practice for the next five minutes. Focus on your body sensations, on staying very relaxed, and on how smooth and easy you can make the book go up and down.

(Pause five minutes.)

When you are at a good stopping place, take your attention off your breathing and rest for a few moments until you are ready to resume your normal activities.

Discussion

Most people can get their breath down into their abdomen the first time. However, if you have been a chest breather for a long time, you may find that you need more practice. I have some of my clients practice this once or twice a day until they get it, and it sometimes takes several weeks. If you find that it takes you a while, be patient with yourself. It is worth it.

ACTIVITY FIVE
Mastering the Learning to Love Yourself Breath

In this activity we will go one step further. Now that you have experienced diaphragmatic breathing lying down, we will try it sitting up. It is easiest to learn lying down, because of gravity, but in order to master it you must be able to breathe effectively sitting up and eventually while moving around.

Instructions
Sit comfortably upright. Rest for a moment with your eyes closed until you are comfortable.

Put your hands on your hips, then slide them up until you can feel the bottom of your rib cage. Slowly tense and relax the muscles of your abdomen. (Be sure to keep your shoulders relaxed—they tend to tense up.) Do this several times, focusing your awareness on the muscles around your navel. Feel the tensing and relaxing with your hands. Make the tensing and relaxing very slow, so that it takes you five seconds or so to tense and five seconds to relax. After you have tensed and relaxed enough to get a clear sense of what it feels like to be tense and relaxed, pause and rest for a minute or so.

Now, relax the muscles of your abdomen as much as you possibly can. Relax them even further. Begin breathing easily in and out, allowing the muscles of your abdomen to stay very relaxed. Breathe deeply and slowly into your belly, feeling the rising and falling of your abdomen with your hands. Continue breathing deeply and slowly into your relaxed abdomen for the next few minutes, feeling your abdomen move with your hands.

(Pause five minutes.)

When you are ready to finish, rest for a few moments before resuming normal activities.

ACTIVITY SIX
Coordinating Breath with Movement

A full, relaxed in breath expands the abdomen so completely that the pelvis makes a slight movement down and back. I have noticed that very few adults can breathe effectively enough to bring about this pelvic movement, although it can readily be seen in a healthy baby. Somewhere along the line we lose the connection between our breathing and our bodies, causing the two to fall out of harmony with each other, and causing us to fall out of love with ourselves and with life. This activity will help you reestablish this vital connection, bringing your breath into synchrony with your movement.

Instructions

Lie down on your back and get comfortable. Bring your knees up so that your feet are flat on the floor. Let your legs be a comfortable foot or so apart.

Breathe slowly and deeply in and out of your relaxed belly. Use your skills of diaphragmatic breathing to let your breath go into your relaxed abdomen.

As you breathe in and your belly fills, arch the small of your back very gently. As you breathe out, flatten the small of your back on the floor. Let the movement be gentle, rolling. It is a very slight arching, just an inch or so. Do it by breathing, not by forcing or tensing your muscles. As you breathe in and arch your lower back, your pelvis rolls down slightly, making room for your breath to go deeply into your low abdomen. As you breathe out, your pelvis rolls back up again. On the in breath, your tailbone rolls down the floor toward its tip. On the out breath your tailbone rolls back up toward the spine.

As you practice this new movement, keep it gentle and easy. Do not push or get impatient. If your lower back feels uncomfortable, make the movement more subtle. Continue practicing now, coordinating the in breath with the arching of the lower back and the out breath with the flattening of the lower back,

(Practice for five to ten minutes.)

When you have reached a good stopping place, rest quietly with your eyes closed for a few moments before resuming normal activities.

Discussion

This activity has great physiological importance. The healthier you become, the more your breath will be in synchrony with the movements of your pelvis. There is a distinct correlation between this synchrony and the ability to love yourself. When your breath is out of harmony with the movements of the rest of your body, you are in conflict with yourself. To give a sad example, I have spent a portion of my working life helping people in mental hospitals. The more regressed the person is, the less

likely he or she is able to breathe in the coordinated
fashion given in the activity above. Many people in the
back wards of mental hospitals have been so traumatized
by life that their breathing is actually moving at odds
with the pelvis. In other words, when they breathe in,
they tighten their bellies and move their pelvises *up*, not
down as one would do in healthy breathing. They are in
mortal combat with themselves twenty thousand times a
day. The people I see in my office every week often have
the same problem to a lesser degree. They are functional
but not making the most of themselves and their potential.

Practice this activity until you master it, and I predict
you will feel better in every cell of your being.

ACTIVITY SEVEN
I Love My Body

This activity comes in two parts. First, you will work
inside yourself in a meditative way. Then you will come
out and work with a partner, if you have one at hand, or
in front of a mirror if you are by yourself. The purpose is
to establish a deeper sense of love for your body.

Instructions
1.   Lie down on your back on a comfortable surface.
Close your eyes and take a moment to relax.

Begin breathing in and out as slowly and deeply as you
can. Be very gentle in your breathing. Keep it relaxed;
do not force the breath. Just breathe as slowly and

deeply as you can comfortably. Do this for a few breaths until you get used to it.

Now, pause for a moment at the top of the in breath and the bottom of the out breath. During each pause, quietly say in your mind, "I love my body," and then feel the love for your body. Breathe again, pause, and repeat. Don't hold your breath in any kind of effortful way. Just take a brief pause at the top and the bottom of the breath, whisper, "I love my body," then give yourself a moment of love. Continue like this for several minutes. When you feel finished, rest for a moment, then go on to the next instruction.

2. Stand facing your partner (or a mirror). Take a full, deep breath, and then say, "I love my body unconditionally." Take another full, deep breath and repeat this statement. Continue until you have said it at least twenty times. Notice any reactions in your mind or body after you have said "I love my body unconditionally." You might feel tension, or your mind might wander, or you might hear some contrary mind chatter. Just notice these things, take another breath, and repeat, "I love my body unconditionally."

CHAPTER 7

Learning to Love Yourself in Relationships

INTRODUCTION: MEETING THE CHALLENGE OF RICHNESS IN RELATIONSHIPS

Relationships have been the source of my most intense discoveries about myself. As I learned to love myself, I would sometimes reach a high state of feeling good, only to create an opportunity in a relationship to fall flat on my face. Relationships are the testing ground, the ultimate proof of our ability to love ourselves. The bright and sometimes harsh searchlight of love will bring to the surface anything in ourselves that we have not loved. That's why relationships afford the greatest opportunity for us to learn to stay centered in our love for ourselves. It is urgent that we learn this lesson, for only by loving ourselves can we really love others. Until you learn to love yourself, you will always be demanding from others what you have not given yourself. Love then becomes need, not celebration.

Here is the challenge. In every human being resides

the twin needs of closeness and independence. We have deep urges to merge with another person, and we have equally strong urges to develop ourselves completely as separate beings. Ideally we would surrender ourselves fully to union with others at the same time that we explore and express our own full potential. But it is not so easy. Many of us are blocked in one or the other of the two dimensions, and sometimes both. In other words, we may not allow ourselves to get close, but we may not allow ourselves to be independent, either. We lock ourselves in an intermediary zone, a psychological purgatory in which we are not in union with others, nor are we autonomous individuals. Week after week I work in therapy with people who cannot be in satisfying relationships with others or themselves. A woman with whom I was working stated the problem very well: "I want to really merge with my husband, but when I do I lose myself. My boundaries disappear and I don't know who I am anymore. I want to be me wherever I am, whether I am by myself or in a relationship. I work so hard to get centered, and then I get close to my husband or even a friend, and I lose my center. Then I get angry and push back. It seems like the only way I know how to define myself is through pushing people away. What I want is to be close to people and be totally me at the same time."

This is what I, too, want. It has taken me two decades of persistent work to learn to be me while being in a relationship. At first I had no idea who I was. My relationships were shadow dances: two illusions interacting with each other. Later I entered my back-and-forth phase. I would get close, then become scared. Out of this fear I would pull back, usually finding fault with the other person. At other times I would get close, then try to control the other person until she got sick of it and left. I did not realize that it was my fear that was driving my obnoxious behavior. I certainly did not see that my fear came from getting close. I thought it actually *was* the other person's fault. I perceived myself a blameless innocent, always being let down or left. One of the biggest breakthroughs of my life came in 1979, when I had a flash of awareness that changed the direction of my life. I saw that it was my problem, not anyone else's. I had a deep fear of being close, born of my difficult early relationship with my mother. My hidden fear was of abandonment. When closeness began to bring that fear to the surface, I would try to control the relationship to keep from being abandoned, or I would imagine that the other person was wrong in order to invalidate her. If I invalidated her first it would not matter if she abandoned me. In any case I would end up alone, secure in my belief: You just can't trust women. But one day I woke up to the humbling awareness that I had dreamed up the whole pattern and had managed to find a dozen or so women to play it out with over and over in my adult life. The awareness led me to dropping this pattern; one month later I met Kathlyn, and the pattern has never surfaced in our relationship.

A great deal of healing needs to take place to allow us to be close, to be ourselves, and to be free. The challenge is awesome, but what else is there to do of value in life? Certainly it is important to be comfortable in your living situation, to make a contribution through your work, and to enjoy yourself through entertainment. But without clarity in close relationships, none of the others means much. I have had the opportunity to work with people as they neared death. Never do they say, "I wish I'd made more money" or "I wish I'd watched more TV." Instead they say things like "I wish I had told my son I loved him" and "I wish I had cleared up my relationship with my mother." Relationships are the central point of existence as we know it on this planet. Let us make the most of them.

This section of the book shows you a number of ways I have used to help people learn to love themselves while in the passion and friction of close relationships.

ACTIVITY ONE
Differentiating Your Feelings
from Your Parents' Feelings

Instructions
I would like you to complete this fill-in-the-blanks letter to your mother. You may use your notebook or a blank sheet of paper. Then I would like you to write another one, to your father. The purpose of the letters is to enhance your ability to discriminate between your feelings and your parents' feelings. It is essential for your growth that you do so, and this letter is a way many people have used to get separate from their parents. People from ages nine to seventy-seven have benefited from this activity.

Dear _____,

I am in the process of learning to love myself. Part of this learning is to separate my feelings from yours. I am doing this out of love for you, and even if I say some things you may not want to hear, please know that I say them out of love for you.

I am both different from you and the same as you. Here are some ways I am different from you. You like _____ , whereas I don't like it at all. You sometimes say _____ , whereas I seldom if ever say that. You feel _____ about _____ , while I don't. I like _____, _____ , and _____ . I have done _____ , which I don't think you have done. You probably wouldn't approve that I have _____ and _____ and even _____ .

But we are alike, too. That's no surprise, since every other cell in my body came from you. For example, I sometimes find myself _____, which is exactly like you. Just like you, I _____ and _____ and even ___ . Some of my best qualities, like _____ , are exactly like the best of you.

Some of my deepest feelings are _____ . Do you share any of those? If I had to guess, I would say that your deepest feelings are _____ .

The reason I say that is that I see you doing the following things: _____ , and that suggests to me how you must feel. When I feel scared, the sensations are _____ . When I feel angry, the sensations are _____ . When I am sad, the sensations are _____ . As I tune in to those feelings in myself, I wonder if you feel them like that.

In closing, I would like to thank you for ___ , and _____ , and especially for _____ . I would not be who I am without you.

Love,

Discussion

Writing this letter helps you begin the process of discriminating your feelings from your parents', a process that will go on throughout your lifetime. Some people who have written the letter have chosen to go ahead and send it. How do you feel about that? Does the idea of actually sending the letter scare you? If so, maybe you should definitely send it. When something triggers fear, you are approaching a growth edge in yourself, something that you might benefit from going through. Whether you send your letter or not, at least you are one step closer to knowing how you feel and intuiting your parents' feelings.

ACTIVITY TWO
What Needs to Be Loved Here?

We will begin our explorations of learning to love yourself in current relationships by tracking your feelings when you are around people. By doing this you will map out the territory of what needs to be loved in yourself. A subsequent activity will build on this fundamental information.

Instructions

This activity asks you to discriminate between two basic feeling states: pleasant/harmonious, and unpleasant/inharmonious. In the first state, you feel pleasant inside and in harmony with those around you. In the second state you feel unpleasant inside and out of harmony with those around you. To help you get in touch with these states so that you can discriminate between them, recall a time when you felt completely happy and at ease inside and with those around you. Remember where you were, what you were doing, and the people you were with. Note how this pleasant, harmonious feeling is experienced in your body. Notice what sensations go along with the feeling of pleasant harmony. Now, to contrast this feeling, think of a time when you felt unpleasant feelings inside, and a disjointed, out-of-harmony feeling with those around you. Remember where you were, what you were doing, and those with whom you were doing it at the time. What made it such a bad experience? Notice how you experience this unpleasant feeling in your body. Where do you feel the unpleasant sensations, and exactly what do they feel like?

Now that you are equipped with a familiarity with these two opposite feeling states, you will be using the information in relationships for one week. During the next week, carry a small notebook or piece of paper with you as you go through your day. Note as often as you can whether you feel pleasant/harmonious or unpleasant/ inharmonious. Make your notes at least once an hour. If possible, note your feeling-state every fifteen minutes. Note also who is around when you are feeling that particular way.

When you have a week's worth of information, go on to the next activity.

ACTIVITY THREE
The Experience of Loving
Your Unpleasant Feelings in Relationships

By now you may have discovered the people and situations that trigger unpleasant feelings in you. It is important to note that these feelings are yours, even though they may have been triggered by others. Because someone else reliably triggers unpleasant feelings in you, you might be tempted to think that the other person causes your feelings. This way of thinking is very dangerous. In reality, *the other person may in a sense be caused by your feelings.* How can this be? In the realm of feelings, a different type of cause and effect may be at work. As an example, let's say that somewhere in your past you have had a painful relationship with your father. Perhaps he was an authoritarian who criticized you or physically abused you. The pain of the feelings you had about him began to color your interactions with all authority figures. Now in your present life you may have a boss who comes in and says, "Where's the Miller file?" Because of your past feelings you may interpret this statement as critical. It triggers a feeling of anger in you, whereas another person would simply say, "Over there on the desk," and remain untriggered. One way to think about it is to picture our past emotional hurts as being like a cocoon or energy field around us. When others are in that field, whatever they do looks like a threat to us, and we may be hypervigilant to their actions. In addition, whenever others are in our field they may find themselves acting in certain ways that fit our preconceptions. The interlock between our emotional field and the people around us cause the feelings we have inside us. We must start by taking responsibility for all our feelings; then we can see more clearly the effect that others have on us.

With all that in mind, let's go on to the specific activity that I have found most useful in learning about this issue. In this experiment, you will have the opportunity to learn to love the unpleasant feelings that others may trigger in you.

Instructions

Jot down several people from your list in whose presence you experienced unpleasant/disharmonious feelings. Jot down several situations that triggered unpleasant/disharmonious feelings. If you did not do the previous activity, right now think of several people and situations that trigger unpleasant feelings in you.

Take the first person from your list and picture the person as vividly as you can. Think about the person until you can feel the unpleasant feeling in your body. Simply sit with this feeling for a moment, giving yourself loving permission to feel it. Love yourself for feeling this way. Do not try to change the unpleasant feeling to something better. Simply love it the way it is. Love the unpleasant sensations as you would someone about whom you care deeply. All your feelings deserve this kind of love; give it to them now. As you love your feelings and sensations, notice whether they change and how they change.

When you are ready to move on, go to the next person or situation on your list. Picture it in your mind and feel it in your body. Let it develop until you can feel the unpleasant feelings that this person or situation triggers in you. When you can feel the unpleasantness, love those sensations just as you would love someone about whom you deeply care. Love them thoroughly, noticing whether they change and how they change.

When you are ready to move on, continue through your list of people and situations that trigger unpleasant sensations in you. Picture each and feel the unpleasant sensations in your body. Love the unpleasantness and notice what happens to it as you do.

When you have reached a stopping place, return to normal activity.

ACTIVITY FOUR
Three Views of Yourself

I mentioned earlier in the book that when I first began to work on myself I was a very different person than I am today: I was a chain-smoking three-hundred-pounder sitting on a powder keg of old anger and other feelings. One of the most important relationships that put me on my growth path was with Dwight Webb, a professor of counseling at the University of New Hampshire. I cannot begin to cover all the changes I initiated through my contact with Dwight, but here are a few: One thing I noticed right away was that Dwight seemed effortlessly in touch with his feelings. From what I could tell, he had no problem admitting when he felt angry or sad or scared or happy. By contrast, I spent much of my energy denying the existence of my feelings. It took me about two seconds to figure out that Dwight's way was better, and I set about the task of reacquainting myself with who I really was inside. Also, Dwight seemed transparent, in the sense that he seemed absolutely uninterested in hiding anything inside himself. This was very different from me; I concealed virtually everything as a matter of course. Dwight invited me to his house one day after I had known him for a couple of months, and I had the opportunity to see him interact with his wife and children. He was utterly the same at home as he was everywhere else! I had grown up among people who changed personalities to fit whomever they were relating to, so to see that Dwight had a kind of absolute relationship integrity deeply moved me. Dwight encouraged me to look at a key issue in my life: the gaps in who I was, what I wanted to be, and how others saw me. I realized that psychological health depended on healing the gaps in these aspects of my life. And there was a monumental gap in my case. First, I did not know much about who I was, and I had certainly never thought about who I wanted to be. I also realized I had constructed my life so that no one really knew who I was.

Looking back, I can see that the next ten years of my life were devoted to healing these gaps. Now I know myself well and am learning more every day. I am who I want to be, doing what I want to do. Perhaps most important, the feedback I get from others is that who I really am is seen by others; they do not perceive a gap. I feel really proud of that, and I am deeply grateful to Dwight (who is alive and well and living in New Hampshire) for turning me 180 degrees and pointing me in a direction that probably saved my life.

I would like you to spend some time considering these issues in a way that may allow you to find out about any gaps that exist in your own life.

Instructions

For this activity you will need three poster boards and a lot of magazines with pictures in them. I would like you to title the three poster boards in the following way: Who I Am, Who I Want to Be, How Others See Me. Go through the magazines (or any other source of pictures) and assemble a collage of pictures that represent Who I Am. On the second poster board do another collage that depicts Who I Want to Be, and depict How Others See Me on the third board.

As you work through these collages, be bluntly honest with yourself. There is nothing to gain by hiding, and much to lose, as I can personally testify. As you complete the collages, ask yourself several questions:

Are there gaps in who I am, who I want to be, and how others see me?

How large are the gaps?
Where did I make the key decisions that put the gaps there?
What do I need to do to heal the gaps?

Love each of your reactions and feelings about this activity. If you feel sad because there is a huge gap between who you are and who you want to be, love yourself for feeling sad. In my original inquiry into these questions back in 1968, there was a 120-pound gap between who I was and who I wanted to be. At first I felt horrible about it, but then I came to feel that it is better to see the truth and go through the pain of it than to continue denying it. Use the activity as an extended exercise in loving yourself for all your reactions.

ACTIVITY FIVE
Confronting the Dragon

Do you have someone in your life who has been a continuing source of anger, anguish, and frustration for you? Another way to ask this question is: Who in your life have you struggled with longest and hardest? Perhaps it is a parent or a spouse, maybe even a child. For the purposes of this activity I want you to think of only one person, although there may be more than one who would fit this category. Without giving her real name and invading her privacy, I would like to give you an example from my own life. Although it has been many years now since I have seen her or talked to her, I can say without hesitation that my relationship with Tania was the most painful of my life. It was stormy from the beginning; both of us were barely out of adolescence chronologically, though our relationship seemed to regress us both instantly to the developmental age of two. We never really got beyond that stage in the four years we were together. We were still fighting about the same things the week we split up that we fought over the first week we met. But the relationship was far from over when we quit being lovers. In fact, some of the worst of it was to come. For some reason we felt compelled to call each other up and excoriate each other at least twice a month for years after we split up. It was bizarre; I can hardly believe now that I ever participated in such a painful situation that had so little positive payoff. However, there was a psychological dynamic at work that I did not know of until much later, a dynamic that kept us locked together in mortal combat even when there was no physical contact between us. The dynamic was projection, and here's how it worked between us: I want to speak entirely now from my own point of view, avoiding any discussion of what her end of the dynamic was. She certainly had her issues, but she can write her own book. For me, the problem was that I had projected my anger completely onto Tania. I would tell people what an angry person she was, and how I had suffered because of her anger. It was very easy to get away with this projection, because practically everyone agreed with me. I got huge amounts of support for being the victim of her anger. But one day I made the observation that this viewpoint, as good as it made me feel, did not seem to help clear up the relationship. I became momentarily humble and asked the universe to reveal to me what was going on. The answer hit me like a bucket of water. I saw that I was disowning my anger completely: I thought that *she* was the angry one in the relationship. In a flash I turned it all around. I opened up to the possibility that she was present in my life to get me to own my anger. She was my anger teacher! I took a deep breath and opened up to all my anger. Years of unexpressed rage shook through my body and streamed through my mind. When I calmed down I said out loud, "I hereby release you from needing to be in my life to teach me about anger." I loved my anger deeply for a moment, then directed love toward her (I aimed it toward the Northeast, where I thought she was!). My whole body felt relieved, as if I were lighter in every cell. I even found myself smiling, with a feeling of genuine regard toward her.

Now here's the part that seems like magic to me. From that moment our relationship changed completely, although I never mentioned my experience of illumination to her. Her calls became infrequent, and when she did call she was uniformly pleasant. After about six more months I never heard from her again, and now the better part of a decade has gone by with no contact between us. Who can be sure that my internal shift was the sole cause of the change? But I can think of no other explanation. In any case, I'll take it gratefully. The lesson I learned in that troubled relationship has now paid off handsomely, with ten years of blessedly conflict-free marriage to Kathlyn.

In this activity you will have the opportunity to move

toward clearing up a chronically painful relationship in your life.

Instructions
Begin by writing the person's name at the top of a sheet of paper. If possible, place a photo of the person along with the name, so that the right hemisphere of your brain will have something to relate to. If no photo is available, make a quick sketch of the person. Working quickly, write down the answers to the following questions.

What is the aspect of him/her that I absolutely can't stand? _____

_____

_____

_____

_____

_____

_____

_____

_____

_____

What is the dominant feeling that I associate with him/her? _____

_____

_____

_____

_____
_____
_____
_____
_____
_____

What did he/she do that I absolutely cannot forgive?

_____
_____
_____
_____
_____
_____
_____
_____
_____

What feelings does he/she trigger in me? (Keep it simple: fear, anger, sadness, sexual arousal.) _____

_____
_____
_____
_____
_____
_____
_____
_____
_____

Complete the following sentences that relate to the person: I'm angry that _____

_____

_____

_____

_____

_____

_____

_____

_____

_____

(Repeat each of these as many times as you can, filling in the blank with something different each time.)

I'm sad that _____.

_____

_____

_____

_____

_____

_____

_____

_____

_____

_____

_____

I'm scared that_____.

_____

_____

_____

_____

_____

_____

_____

_____

_____

I'm sexually attracted to _____ . I'm not sexually attracted to _____ .

(Write *both* of these, noticing what feelings come up in your body as you do.)

Now that you have some basic information on the table about your relationship with this person, let's go into a more advanced area.

How is what you cannot stand about this person something that you absolutely must learn about yourself?

_____

_____

_____

_____

_____

_____

_____

_____

_____

How is the dominant feeling of this person something that you must learn to handle in yourself? _____

_____

_____

_____

_____

_____

_____

_____

Assume for a moment that we invite people into our lives to help us learn a lesson that we could not learn any other way. What lesson did you need to learn from him/her that you might not have been able to learn any other way?

What need did this person meet in your life when you first encountered him/her? (This need may be something you are not proud of. For example, I can now see that Tania filled a need in me to have a way of avoiding dealing with my grief over my grandmother's death, which had happened just before I met Tania.) _____

_____

_____

_____

_____

_____

_____

_____

What need is she/he still meeting in your life? _____

_____
_____
_____
_____
_____
_____
_____
_____
_____
_____
_____

Are you willing to release this person from playing this painful role in your life? In other words, are you willing to learn the lessons you've been learning from him/her in some other way? _____

_____
_____
_____
_____
_____
_____
_____
_____
_____
_____
_____
_____

Are you willing to heal this relationship? _____

_____

_____

_____

_____

_____

_____

_____

_____

Are you willing now to forgive yourself and him/her for bringing one another so much pain? _____

_____

_____

_____

_____

_____

_____

_____

_____

Discussion

It may be valuable for you to go through these questions several times, because your mind and body will probably generate a fresh set of responses each time. I have used these questions with many relationships of my own, and I have given them to clients in therapy to help heal hundreds of their painful interlocks. Give yourself time and patience as you use these questions, as they are likely to stir up feelings you might not know you had about the person. If you are sincerely interested in clearing up the relationship, however, eventually these questions will point you in a healing direction.

ACTIVITY SIX
Healing Your Wounded Inner Child

As I work with people in therapy week after week, helping them heal troubled relationships, I repeatedly see that the cause of much of the disharmony is the shy, wounded child that most of us carry within us. Hidden deep inside us is a part that retreated from the world long ago. It decided the world was not safe, that life was a place where there was no possibility of getting its needs met. In close relationships, these inner children come to the fore, often to do battle with each other. What looks like a painful relationship between adults is more like a duel between two hurting children. Often I have concluded, after a day of working with people, that there is no such thing as a grown-up.

The wounded child has only two approaches to problem solving: implode or explode. When the stress is on, our Inner Child tries to hide even more, or it strikes out in fury. By now I have seen many combinations of relationships: two hiders, one hider and one striker, two strikers. None of these patterns works, because both striking out and hiding mask an authentic revealing of the shared pain of the old wounds. I am always deeply moved when two people have the courage to surrender their wounded-child strategies and face the fact that both are hurting and confused. When hot words and frozen silences melt down into a confession of mutual pain, I know that a deep healing is about to occur. Unfortunately, however, the wounds are sometimes so deep that I cannot find a way to invite out one or both of the hidden children inside. Then I feel sad because I know what it is like to carry around the burden of a hurting, hidden entity inside me. The relationship I mentioned earlier, with Tania, was a classic example of two struggling wounded children. Looking back on it, there was never any encounter between the two authentic people that we really were. All our interactions and entanglements were the struggles between two hurting, sometimes hating, children.

It does not have to be that way. With much work, I was able to make friends with the wounded child who was so often in control of my interactions with people. I learned to know what he felt like, what he needed, and what he needed to say. With practice and patience, I learned to communicate with him, so that I could use my adult skills and knowledge to meet his ancient needs. Now we are friends, and he no longer needs to use his whines and temper tantrums to get my attention. I would like to share with you a beginning way for you to contact your Inner Child. Perhaps this activity will inspire you to take on a deeper journey of healing this hidden part of you. Many resources exist to help you. Charles Whitfield has written an excellent book by the title of *Healing the*

Child Within, and he also has recently written a work-book of activities called *A Gift to Myself*. Also still available is Hugh Missildine's classic *Your Inner Child of the Past*, a book that is as fresh and useful now as it was when first published.

Our activity will focus on the feelings of the wounded Inner Child as you experience them in your body. My experience has been that these nagging old feelings are what really need to be transformed. Once you feel better inside, it is easier to make changes outside. Much of this activity is done with your eyes closed, so it is preferable to have a friend guide you through it. If you are by yourself, an alternative is to tape-record the instructions and play them back to yourself.

Instructions
Sit comfortably, and close your eyes. Rest for a few moments inside yourself until you are relaxed and ready to proceed.

You are going to develop a dialogue now with your Inner Child. This is the part of you that remembers all the feelings of being a child growing up in the world around you. Your Inner Child is the repository of all the things that happened to you while you were growing up: humiliation, joy, fear, creativity, heartbreak, spontaneity, and all the other positive and negative feelings you experienced in your childhood. Sit back now, and spend some time getting to know your Inner Child.

Recall a time in your childhood when you felt completely safe and secure. . . . Remember where you were . . . what you were doing . . . how you felt inside. This feeling will be your safe place to come back to throughout this activity. Now and then as we go through the instructions, you will be asked to return to your safe and secure feeling. Get a good sense of it now in your body, so that you can return to it later on.

Let's give your Inner Child a name. It could be a name you were called as a child, or a new name you make up for it now. Just let a name come into your mind by which you can call your Inner Child in this activity. When you have a name, go on.

Make contact now with your Inner Child. Say, "I want to make friends with you, _____, so I can feel better and more loving to myself. Are you willing to be friends?" When you get a yes, move on. If you don't get a yes, find out why your Inner Child is not willing to be friends.

If you are good at visualizing, get a picture of your Inner Child in your mind. See how he or she is dressed, how big the Child is, and what body language, emotional tone come through in your vision of him or her. After you have done this, return to your safe and secure feeling for a few moments.

Tune in to the dominant feeling tone of your Inner Child. Scared? Angry? Sad? Happy? Confused? All of these? Select one feeling that you can call your dominant feeling tone of your Inner Child. Tune in to this feeling now in your body. Notice if it is still exactly the way it was when you were a child, or if there has been a change in it. Notice how and where it shows up in your body right now. After you have done this, return to your safe and secure feeling for a few moments.

Now think of the most difficult and stressful interactions you have in your current life. Which people are the most difficult for you to relate to? What situations trigger the most uncomfortable feelings in you? After you have thought of several situations and people, ask yourself honestly, "Are these situations and people really bringing forth my Inner Child? Do I disappear in these situations, leaving my Inner Child to interact with others?" After you get your answer, return to your safe and secure feeling for a few moments.

Now breathe into your safe and secure feeling, letting it expand throughout your body. Relax your arms and legs, allowing your safe and secure feeling to spread down into your legs and out into your arms. When you are feeling an expanded sense of safety and security in your body, get in touch with your dominant Inner Child feeling. When you can feel it, surrender it and let it melt down into your safe and secure feeling. Let your safe and secure feeling receive your Inner Child feeling completely. Continue until you feel only the safe and secure feeling all over your body.

When you feel that the process is complete, slowly open your eyes and resume normal activity.

Discussion

Many people who do this activity report the discovery that their wounded Inner Child has been running their lives. Without realizing it, they have been connecting to the world through the feelings of the Inner Child. For example, you may think you are talking to your boss, but really it's your Inner Child who's having the conversation. That's the bad news. The even worse news is that practically everyone else is doing the same thing. We have a world full of wounded children trying to act like grown-ups. The first step in healing this problem is to recognize it, to get acquainted again with our Inner Child, and learn to give it the expression it needs.

If you would like to go further with the exploration of your Inner Child, here is a suggestion that many of my clients have used. Spend a little time each day giving your Inner Child a chance to express himself or herself. My wife, Kathlyn, has discovered that her Inner Child loves to paint. She sets aside a little time every day to give her Child an opportunity to express herself this way. She has a room set up in our house for painting, and I'm frequently amazed when I stick my head into the room to see a powerful new painting springing forth. It is the creative inquiry that is important to her, not the end product. In fact, her artwork is centered around asking herself the question "What color do I feel like using, and where would I like to put it?" In addition, both of us have found that our Inner Children love to dance and move; nearly every day we set aside time for spontaneous, creative dancing. The rules are simple: Turn on some music and move to it. We don't practice any particular dance form; rather, the important thing for us is to ask, "How does my body want to move right now?" One of my heroes, Ashley Montague, is still vibrant in his eighties. One of his secrets is that he dances an hour a day, whether or not he has a partner. Whether your Child likes to paint or dance or whittle or toss a baseball, you owe it to him or her to create a chance to play every day. Try it, and see if you don't notice an overall lightening of the spirit.

ACTIVITY SEVEN
Feeling Conversations

Our feelings are communicated through our bodies: tone of voice, gestures, breathing patterns, muscles that extend or tighten, and other nonverbal cues. When we listen to what people are saying to us, we are primarily tuned in to *how* they are saying what they are saying. Is their body language congruent with their word language? Human beings have developed sophisticated ways of recognizing deception, and equally sophisticated ways of pretending we don't notice when the other person is lying. It may be that we are losing this skill, now that several generations have grown up seeing so many professional liars in the form of TV actors and product spokespersons. As Sir Laurence Olivier was said to have stated: "The secret of acting is honesty; once I learned how to fake that, I had it made."

Human beings have been trying to reconcile their words with their actions for a long time, and not always with success. In relationships, we have to look at a key issue: Is our intention to reveal or to conceal? In other words, is your participation in this relationship coming out of a desire to uncover yourself and your feelings fully, or are you here to hide? If your intention is to reveal yourself completely, your experience of close relationships will be much smoother; you will not be wasting energy through rehearsing, editing, and revising your thoughts and actions. This activity will give you the opportunity to explore all the territory beneath and beyond words. Preferably, find a partner for this activity. In a pinch, a full-length mirror will do.

Instructions

1. Stand facing your partner. Take turns completing the sentence "Right now I feel _____." Say whatever word or feeling pops into your mind to fill in the blank. Exchange three turns.

2. Next, complete the sentence "Right now I feel _____," and when it comes time to fill in the blank, express the feeling through your body language and gestures *only*, no words. Exchange three turns.

3. Now, complete the sentence "Right now I feel _____," filling in the blank with gestures and body language, but make them much larger than life. Act them out very dramatically. Exchange five turns, then pause for discussion.

Discussion

Feelings are always flowing through us. In this activity you are opening the window and noticing what is passing by. Sometimes you may feel blank when it comes time to fill in the blank; go ahead and make a gesture that means "nothing" or "blank." Even subtle feelings can be expressed through body language. Naturally some people are better at expressing themselves nonverbally than others. In many relationships the very problem at stake is one or both person's lack of ability to express feelings. The technical name for this problem is alexithymia, which comes from a Greek word that means "no word for mood." Many of the activities in this book can be considered specific treatments for alexithymia, which some people consider the disease of our time.

ACTIVITY EIGHT
Tracing Your Body in Relationships

This activity, a slightly more advanced version of something you have done already, is to assist you in owning
and loving more of yourself. This is a valuable activity to
repeat again and again over time, because it allows you
to see visually the progress you have made in learning to
love yourself. You will need a piece of paper a little
bigger than you are. Newspaper endrolls are good, as is
butcher paper. You'll also need crayons, markers, or pas-
tels, and a partner.

Instructions

1. Spread out a length of paper that is taller than one
of you. The person to be traced will lie down on the
paper. You can choose your position: open, curled up,
arms and legs splayed, however you feel like expressing
yourself. Your partner then traces the outline of your
body with a marker, pastel, or crayon. When finished,
switch roles and trace the other person.

2. Now find several colors that you like and several
that you don't like. Use the colors you like to color in the
areas of your body that you feel are lovable. Tune in to
the shapes, sensations, and textures of those areas as
you color. Be as exact as you can. For example, you may
discover that you experience a thin line of unlovability
only in your upper arms, not the whole arm. Use the
colors you dislike to fill in the areas of your body you feel
are unlovable. Those areas are places where you feel
active dislike, blankness, numbness, or less aliveness.

3. When you have finished coloring, show your body tracing to your partner and share your discoveries.

4. Taking turns, place your hand on an unlovable part of your partner's body. Actively love that part while your partner repeats aloud, "I'm willing to love this part of me." Take as long as you need until the person feels a perceptible shift in that part of their body. The shift could be relaxation, greater awareness, love, or some other reaction. When finished with one place, go on to another until both of you have completed all the places you colored unlovable.

Discussion

Many people discover through this activity just how distorted their body image is. They look at their tracing and say, "That's not what I look like!" The lack of love for a given part of ourselves actually warps our ability to see it clearly the way it is. As one participant in a workshop put it, "I thought this part was awful and huge, and now that I see all the beautiful parts of me that surround it, they seem to invite this part into a field of love."

ACTIVITY NINE
Eliminating Codependence from Your Close Relationships

The problem of codependence has undergone a meteoric rise in the public consciousness over the past decade. I have been asked what codependence is so many times by the media and members of the interested public that I have often thought of having a T-Shirt printed with my favorite definitions on it. If I were to have such a shirt made, it would say on it things like:

- Codependence is feeling someone else's feelings instead of your own.
- Codependence is being the caretaker of everyone but you.
- Codependence is being entangled with someone in a relationship in which both of you experience less freedom and creativity than you had before.
- Codependence is allowing your life to be run by someone else.
- Codependence is occurring when your life is unmanageable by being in a relationship with someone whose life is unmanageable.

People whose lives are marred by codependence do not have relationships, they have entanglements. An entanglement is defined as "a snare or trap from which escape is difficult." Another definition is "when two things are enfolded upon each other so that the freedom of each is limited." Regardless of how you define it, codependence is pain. I urge you to examine the growing literature on codependence; Melody Beattie's books *Codependent No More* and *Beyond Codependency* are excellent introductions to the subject. If you wish to go further, my wife and I have written *Conscious Loving: The Journey to Co-Commitment*. Our book describes a winning alternative to the losing proposition of codependence.

In this activity we undertake a key step in overcoming codependence: the separation of our own feelings from the feelings of others.

Instructions

Begin by making a list of several people with whom you have difficult, entangled involvements. Who do you find yourself worrying about a lot? Whose behavior concerns you? Who in your life affects you such that when they are upset, it is hard for you to stay centered and in harmony? Jot down as many of those people as you can think of.

Now sit comfortably for a moment, closing your eyes and relaxing inside. Pick the person from your list with whom you have the most troubled relationship. Think of the person in your mind, picturing them in whatever way you are able. Notice what the person is wearing. Notice from which angle you are viewing the person. As you picture the person, tune in to the sensations of your own body. Particularly, feel where your boundaries overlap. Notice where you are bound together in an overinvolved sense.

As soon as you have a good sense of the places in your body where you are overinvolved with the person, choose some means of disconnecting from him or her. For example, you could sever the connection, or let it melt, or step back from the person. Do whatever feels correct for you. As you disconnect, notice the feeling(s) in your body that emerge from separating and letting the person be separate. Do you feel discomfort? fear? sadness? relief? Just notice what emerges. This information tells you why you have been overinvolved with the person.

Ask yourself quietly in your mind: Am I willing to let this person live his or her own life? Am I willing to let this person feel his or her own feelings? Am I willing to let this person make his or her own mistakes and learn from them? Am I willing to be separate from him or her? Just notice your answers and the reactions of your body. There are no right or wrong answers here, simply whatever is true for you.

Finally, picture in your mind an image of the person as completely whole, free, and autonomous. Feel yourself as completely whole, free, and autonomous. Notice any reactions you have to both of you being free, whole, and autonomous. Get comfortable with both of you existing in the same space, but completely free of each other.

When you feel complete, end the activity or repeat with another person from your list.

Discussion

This is a simple activity with great power and potential. I encourage you to take the principles of the activity into all parts of your life. Look for where you are overinvolved. See what you need to do to end these unhealthy connections, so that you can be absolutely free while treating others as absolutely free and equal too. This task is not an easy one, by any means. By the time most of us wake up in adulthood, we have surrounded ourselves with a network of people with whom we are overinvolved. But we must begin somewhere. Take a small step each day toward liberating yourself and others from the bondage of codependence, and you will be rewarded with better relationships than you ever imagined.

Epilogue:
The Farther Reaches
of Loving Yourself

How good are you willing to feel? Would it be all right
with you to live in a continuous state of positive energy?
If this is what you really want, I think you will find some
of the following ideas of value. They are concepts that
have meant a great deal to me over the years of my most
intense personal development. When I think back over
the breakthrough moments of loving myself that have
really advanced my evolution, I see them falling into
several main categories. I would like to discuss these
awarenesses with you, in hopes that they will shed light
on your own evolution.

EQUALITY

I am grateful to Thaddeus Golas, author of my favorite
book, *The Lazy Man's Guide to Enlightenment*, for the
first words of his first chapter: "We are equal beings and
the universe is our relations with each other. The uni-

verse is made of one kind of entity: Each one is alive, each determines the course of his own existence." I have thought of this idea thousands of times since I first read it in 1971, and it has helped me work out nearly every problem I have ever encountered in my personal growth. Every moment you and I are faced with a choice: to be responsible or not. Thaddeus's two sentences seem to me the ultimate statement of freedom and responsibility. Almost every day I find myself having a deeper understanding of how I am responsible for creating my life. As a result I feel more free every day.

Perceiving myself as an equal being in a world of other equal beings brought a great relief to me. For much of my life I saw myself as a victim, a person with no power against the persecutors. From the victim position, everyone looked like a potential persecutor, so I stayed in a state of hypervigilance: Who would be on my case next? Finally I began to wake up to the awareness that I had imposed this view of the world on the world, not vice versa. I began to ask myself: What would the world and my life look like if I saw myself as responsible for creating it? Instead of seeing myself as a nail in a world of hammers, could I get beyond victim and persecutor to feel equal? This question shook up my whole world view, causing me to examine every area of my life. I realized that in all my close relationships I either played the victim or the persecutor role. I even put my then-toddler daughter in one of those roles: One day I would see her as a victim, the next day as my persecutor. Sometimes I would play the role of the rescuer, which of course required a victim to rescue. I was horrified to see what a mess of inequality pervaded my life.

I got out of the game. I stopped playing victim and started taking responsibility for my life. I put myself on a strict projection diet: Whenever I would find myself attributing the cause of my problems to someone out there, I would pull it back in here. One thing that happened right away was that all my relationships either changed for the better or fell apart. This was painful, because some of my oldest relationships were based entirely on shared victimhood, and these dropped away quickly. The positive payoff was that the few close relationships that remained were based on each person being responsible for him or herself. Now I think that these relationships are the only ones that deserve to be called relationships; everything else is an entanglement.

Perceiving myself as equal to others and responsible for the course of my existence actually solved most of my problems with people. You see, it is not possible to have a power struggle between two people who each take complete responsibility for their lives. Without power struggles, relationships either get better in a hurry or dissolve equally quickly. Over the years I have seen over one thousand couples in some stage of a troubled relationship, and there has been a power struggle in effect *every time*. I am often overwhelmed by the transformation of a couple when each partner takes complete responsibility and drops the power struggle. Sometimes they are literally hard to recognize when they come in the next week. Light has replaced the dullness in the eyes, and on dozens of occasions there has been a rapid loss of excess weight. Once an overweight man dropped thirty-seven pounds between sessions right after dropping his victim position.

When we fully understand that we are equal beings in a world of equals, a great burden drops from our psyches. When we are victims in a world of persecutors, or when we are struggling back and forth between the two positions, there is little opportunity for learning. We greet each moment with an indignant attitude: "*This* isn't the experience I'm supposed to be having." When we understand the universe as a product of relationships between equals and feel as if we are one of these equals, we are free to greet each moment as an opportunity to learn about ourselves and the world. Without the power struggle of victim and persecutor, genuine possibilities open up for finding out what is really going on in a troubled relationship situation.

Let me give you an example of how this works. A woman came to Kathlyn and me for therapy. She had suffered much abuse as a child, growing up in a small Texas oil town with an alcoholic, authoritarian father and a mother who was sick much of the time. Her father was alternatively seductive or physically abusive, depending on what state of drunkenness he was in. Now, we do not need to put one second of analysis into why she was in that family with that particular mother and father: That's just what life handed her. However, when she came in for therapy it was because she and her otherwise gentle boyfriend had had a blowup in which he had pushed her around. At first she was totally enmeshed in the victim position: "I trusted him so much! How could he do a thing like that!" After she ventilated her anger, she had an earthshaking realization. It was that she had been part of several other situations in which someone she trusted had suddenly become abusive. Any Psych 101 student could point out the obvious, that she was creating replays of her childhood trauma. Why had she not seen it before? She realized that she had not seen the obvious because all her energy had gone into perpetuating the victim/persecutor roles in her relationships. As she would get close to someone she would begin to erect subtle and not-so-subtle defenses, always on the lookout for her boundaries to be invaded. Her expectation was that people were going to transform into persecutors, so that is what she got. You have heard the old saying, I'll believe it when I see it. The opposite is also true: We'll see it when we believe it. She came into relationships with the belief that she would be victimized, and she was.

I certainly am not saying that victims and persecutors do not exist in the real world. I have worked with too many battered children ever to say a thing like that. Despite what all the psychics and occultists say, I think the notion that we choose our parents is ridiculous. Who would choose a normal prenatal life, only to become brain-damaged because of lack of oxygen at birth? Who would choose a cocaine-addicted mother or a drunken father who beat you? As an aside, I can tell you that I have had as clients a number of famous channels and psychics, and their problems are just as rooted in the pain of this present life as yours and mine are. Every single psychic with whom I have worked has gotten healthy only after learning to focus on present pain, feelings and issues, not on anything in a past life.

The truly interesting questions are, Why am I creating my life the way it is? and Am I willing to take responsibility for creating it more the way I want it? Every second that is wasted through pleading victim or being the persecutor could be better spent figuring out how you would like your life to be. I was around thirty before I began to see that my life was a design problem. My job was to figure out what I wanted and design a way to get there. Even now under stress I find myself slipping into the role of victim, and what always pulls me out is remembering to ask myself simple questions like "How would I like it to be?" and "What do I want?"

ONENESS

Nearly every major breakthrough of my own journey has brought me into a greater sense of oneness with myself or the world. In life we begin in a flash of oneness; then our cells divide. In our prenatal lives we spend nine months in oneness, then are born into separation. We are one with the breast, then separate into autonomy. We separate ourselves from our feelings only to have to come back into unity with them in order to feel happy and whole. We project separateness onto those around us only to find that life works best when we embrace others and feel one with them. Oneness and duality permeate our lives; the universe itself is always in the process of being one and becoming two, only to become one again.

The illusion of separation causes a great deal of pain in human life. The illusion is compelling; after all, it is clear that we live in separate skins. This fact of life becomes generalized, and we begin to feel that these skins are islands separated from others by a large gulf. But I have found that I am more connected to myself and others than I ever imagined. Early in my life I separated myself from important parts of myself, chiefly my feelings. I became numb to my anger, my fear, and my sadness, living in the cool world of my beliefs and opinions. My feelings truly did become islands within me, on the other side of a vast gulf of unconsciousness. As within, so without. I placed the same gulf between me and others, then erected a whole philosophy around the virtues of self-reliance. It took a great deal of work to cross the gulf and reconnect myself to my feelings and to other people.

Now, after working with people for twenty-some years, I have abundant evidence that we are much more tuned in to each other than we pretend. As my own evolution progressed I began to develop telepathy, although I hesitate to use the word because it sounds much too mysterious and special. I now believe that all of us are telepathic but that we turn off this skill in the growing-up process. Here is an example of the kind of telepathy I have come to rely upon: One day I was listening to a woman talk about some of her issues, and suddenly the odd thought popped into my mind that she had seen a dead person early in her life. The thought was particularly strange because she was talking about something that had just happened the day before. I blurted out, "Did you have a traumatic experience with a dead person when you were a kid?" She burst into tears and told me of a time when she had found a man in a ditch and had run home to tell her parents she had found a dead man. Everybody had ridiculed her, leaving her a deep impression that she could not trust anyone. Finally she convinced them that she wasn't making it up, and the family trooped out to see the man. It turned out that the man was only dead drunk, and then her family made a joke of it for a long time. It was the beginning of a long script for her of trying to be helpful and having it go unappreciated, which related to the very issue she was describing to me in the first place. Where had the idea of the dead man come from? Obviously from her storehouse of memories. How did it get from her head into mine? Nobody knows. This example is but one of dozens that remind me often that I do not stop at my own skin. I am not only intimately connected with other human beings but also with the universe itself. How can it be otherwise? The illusion of separation would have us believe that we are something different from the universe. Thinking we are separate makes us roam the world as lone wolves or propels us to mesh our boundaries with others' in unhealthy ways. But a moment's clear insight gives us the obvious: We are the same thing as everything else in the universe. As Lewis Thomas points out, the universe looks most like one big cell. All parts of a cell must have some form of rudimentary contact with each other. So telepathy may be an essential form of communication that nature devised a long time ago. Now, the telephone and the fax machine may be more reliable, but they are surely not as satisfying. I find great satisfaction and relief in knowing that we are all communicating with each other on levels we may not know about.

Oneness with ourselves brings happiness; oneness with others brings harmony and bliss to our interactions. Oneness with the universe, with the higher source of creation of the world, brings an expanded, exalted sense of spiritual well-being that makes every moment of life richer. I had my first moment of universal oneness in the mid-1970s, and several years passed before I had another. Now, with the benefit of another decade's work on myself, I experience these moments much more frequently. Often now they come in clusters over several days, followed by another wave a few days later. Frequently I feel them at the end of meditation (I meditate for about half an hour twice a day), and also often when I am by myself in nature. Who knows why they come as they do or why they do not come for a few days or a week? All I know is that I plan to keep meditating and breathing and walking in nature, because for me these rushes of oneness with the universe are among my most treasured moments. As the Archbishop of Canterbury once said, "When I pray, miracles happen. When I don't, they don't." I feel the same way about my meditation and breathing practices. When I started setting aside an hour or so a day for them, miracles began happening in my life. Now I feel like I live on such a steady diet of miracles that life itself seems like a constant unfolding miracle.

I am sure that these miracles were happening all around me and trying to happen through me long before I decided to participate with them. As I learned to be with myself more through meditation and relaxation and breathing practices, I found that what was really happening was that I was dropping my resistance. At first I felt naked without it. Resistance was a dominant theme of my life. I resisted contact with myself, closeness with others, communion with the universe. I made a virtue of resistance. As I tracked down the source of the problem, I found that it ultimately had to do with my resistance to my mother when I was a baby. I had developed a style of resisting my mother's energy, and then had generalized this style to the rest of life. Now I began to see that I had a choice. I did not need to impose this old pattern onto my whole world. Barriers began to melt, and I began to experience more love and energy than I had ever felt. As I became comfortable living without resistance, I found that the naked feeling was replaced by a sense of freedom. As my energy was less consumed by resistance I found I had more juice to fuel my creative projects. Life began to move at a faster, more productive pace.

SOURCING

Along with the realizations of equality and oneness came a truly beautiful concept that has now become the ground of my being. I realized that I had lived most of my life as a consumer of love and positive energy, not as a producer. I sought love through manipulation, and self-esteem through the approval of others. It never seemed to work; I never really felt loved, and the approval I got seemed to go down a bottomless pit. My growth took a giant leap as I began to see that my job was to be a source of love, not to demand it from others. Trying to get it came from the ground-floor assumption that I didn't have it. As long as this assumption was in place, I could never get it from others, either. One of the great lessons to be learned here on earth is to give ourselves the love we demand from others. I now feel that my task here is to turn others on to the power and potential of loving themselves. I want to be a producer, not a consumer, because the producer always has plenty. It is actually the most abundant place to be. In human life, I have found that an odd principle seems to hold sway: What I focus my attention on seems to expand. When I formerly focused on what I did not have, what I did not have grew and expanded! I felt as though I had even less. As I consumed myself with getting others to love me and confirm that I was OK, my feelings of self-hate and worthlessness grew even larger. Somewhere along the line I changed my focus toward how I could be the source of it for others. My intent became to feel love for me and to generate a space in which others could feel love and self-esteem. As if by magic, love and self-esteem grew in abundance. I recommend this point of view to you without reservation. I have been teaching this principle for many years now, and I have never had any dissatisfied customers ask for their scarcity back.

THE EXPANDING UNIVERSE OF LOVE

Scientists tell us that the universe is expanding at an awesome rate. That is probably why we humans get so unhappy so quickly when we try to stand still. Have you noticed that if you try to quit growing you get stiff and fat and sluggish and paranoid? Nobody knows where the universe is expanding from and where it is expanding to, but I have proved to my own satisfaction that if I resist expanding I get miserable and when I participate with expansion I get happy. So I have concluded that it helps to do what the rest of the universe is doing. If I separate myself from others and resist growing, the universe does not seem to be bothered but I seem to have a bad time. So I have said good-bye to resistance. I have dedicated my life to learning what I need to learn in each moment, to seeing everything and everyone as a teacher, to using every life situation as an opportunity to expand my ability to love.

Perhaps the whole universe is doing what we are doing: expanding away from the contraction of self-hate to the all-encompassing space of love. It is delicious to conceive of all of us participating in a universal process of opening to love. Why not see it this way? Everyone is entitled to a view of the universe, since we are all equal beings, and I'll stack this view against any others I've heard so far. Regardless of what the cosmos is doing, however, I have personally felt the liberation that love brings. I have winced from the pain of separation, and I have tasted the sweet relief of becoming one again. From a lifetime of working to transform my own life and the lives of others, I now know something precious: Life is only real when I love. As I write these words I feel the union of love and truth inside myself, and my body glows with the joy that this union brings. I feel very blessed to know and experience these things.

May your journey be equally blessed.

Index

Made in the USA
San Bernardino, CA
27 January 2018